TIGERS, DURBARS
AND KINGS

TIGERS, DURBARS AND KINGS

Fanny Eden's Indian Journals

1837–1838

Transcribed and Edited by

JANET DUNBAR

John Murray

Frontispiece: Fanny Eden by F. Rochard, 1835.
Private collection. Photograph courtesy of The National
Portrait Gallery

Fanny Eden's Journals © India Office Library and Records 1988
Introduction, linking passages and editorial matter © Janet Dunbar 1988

First published 1988
by John Murray (Publishers) Ltd
50 Albemarle Street, London, W1X 4BD

Printed and bound in Great Britain
by Butler & Tanner Ltd, Frome

British Library Cataloguing in Publication Data
Eden, Fanny
  Tigers, durbars and kings: Fanny Eden's
  Indian journals, 1837–1838.
  1. India——Description and travel——
  1762–1858
  I Title   II. Dunbar, Janet.
  915.4′04314′0924   DS412

ISBN 0-7195-4440-8

for Lysbeth

Acknowledgements

I wish first to express my grateful thanks to Dr R. J. Bingle, of the India Office Library, for his help in making Fanny Eden's Journals available to me. I must also make formal acknowledgement to the India Office Library and Records for permission to publish the Journals. Lysbeth Merrifield was very helpful throughout, and Eileen Ward gave up much time to necessary checking. I also wish to thank Linda Silvester for assistance in the early stages of the transcription.

Where necessary, the Journals have been punctuated and paragraphed. Ellipses indicate the occasional indecipherable word or phrase, or passages omitted because they refer to postal details or to drawings not included here. Fanny's spelling of Indian place names and words has not been altered. Her drawings have been left uncaptioned in nearly all cases. Their position is indicated in square brackets in the text when they do not appear on the same page as or opposite her reference to them.

Contents

Who's Who

George: George Eden, Lord Auckland (1784–1849). Appointed Governor-General of India in 1835.

Emily: Emily Eden (1797–1869), sister of Lord Auckland.

Fanny: Frances Eden (1801–1849), sister of Lord Auckland.

William: The Hon. William Godolphin Osborne. Military Secretary to Lord Auckland as well as being his nephew. Became Lord William Osborne in 1859 when his brother succeeded to the Dukedom of Leeds.

William Macnaghten: Government Secretary to Lord Auckland.

Mr Torrens: assistant to William Macnaghten.

Major Byrne: Political Secretary, assistant to Lord Auckland.

John Russell Colvin: Private Secretary to Lord Auckland.

Captain Cunningham
      MacGregor
      Macintosh   } Aides-de-Camp
      Nicholson

Captain Hawkins: in charge of victualling the camp.

Dr Drummond: medical attendant to the party.

Mr Wimberley: chaplain.

Colonel John Lowe: Resident at Lucknow, the capital of the kingdom of Oude (Oudh).

Runjeet (Ranjit) Singh: Ruler of the Sikh Empire.

Dost Mohamed (Mohammed): Ruler of Afghanistan, deposed by British.

Shah Soojah (Shuja): ex-Ruler of Afghanistan, reinstated by the British.

Myra: Fanny's ayah.

Jones: Fanny's English maid.
Dulhoo: Hindu steward attached to Lord Auckland's party.
Ariffe: 'the Musselman jemadar'
Gazelle: Fanny's pet deer.
Rolla: Fanny's lemur (actually a loris).
Chance: Emily's spaniel.
Rosencrantz and Guildenstern: Macintosh and Nicholson.

Glossary

Ayah	Indian lady's maid or nursemaid.
Babu	an English-speaking Bengali.
Begum	a Mohammedan lady of rank.
Bhawani	Kali, Goddess of Destruction.
Chaddar	native dress; a sheet.
Chota	small.
Chobdar	stick-bearer. Attendant or an official of rank, who carries a stick overlaid with silver. Fanny often mentions 'silver-sticks' when referring to these officials.
Chourie	yak's tail set in a handle and used as a fly-whisk.
Dacoit	robber belonging to an armed gang.
Dak	transport by relays of men or horses. Also the Post.
Dhuli	covered litter.
Ghaut (ghat)	landing place.
Hackery	bullock cart.
Havildar	sepoy non-commissioned officer: a sergeant.
Jeel	a mere or lagoon.
Jemadar	chief servant. Also rank of native officer in a company of sepoys, below a Subadar and above a Havildar.
Jonpaun	chair like a sedan-chair with two poles, borne on sticks between the poles, for use in hilly districts.
Khansama	chief table servant.
Kitmutgar	Mohammedan servant who waits at table under the Khansama.
Lac (of rupees)	£10,000.
Mahout	elephant driver.
Mali	gardener.
'Murray'	Fanny probably heard the word 'mara', meaning 'hit', when the beaters shouted that a tiger had been hit. She deduced wrongly that the word was synonymous with 'carcase'.

Nautch	a dance performed by girls and women, a usual princely entertainment.
Nazir	a kind of Court sheriff ('George's chief servant').
Palanquin	a litter for one, borne on poles carried on men's shoulders. Emily described is as 'nothing but a bed in a box'.
Punkah	a large fan, formed of cloth stretched on a rectangular frame, suspended from the ceiling and pulled by a servant using an attached cord.
Ranee	a Hindu queen.
Sepoy	Indian soldier in British service.
Sirdar	a chief or leader.
Suttee	rite of wife-burning on the death of a husband; all the wives, by age-old custom, ascended the husband's funeral pyre and were burnt to death.
Syce	groom.
Thanadar	village headman.
Thugs	devotees of Kali, the Goddess of destruction, whose worship took the form of ritually strangling travellers. The hereditary cult was being suppressed by the British at this time.
Tilbury	a two-wheeled carriage.
Tonjaun, Tonjon	portable chair carried like a palanquin by a single pole and four bearers.

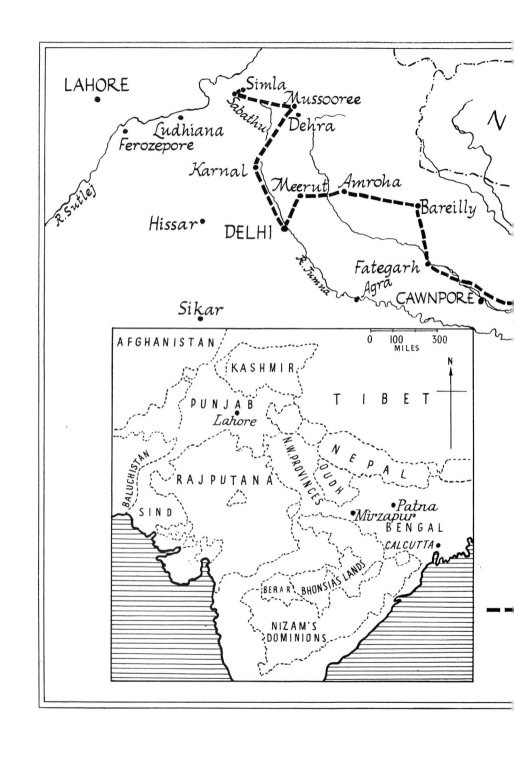

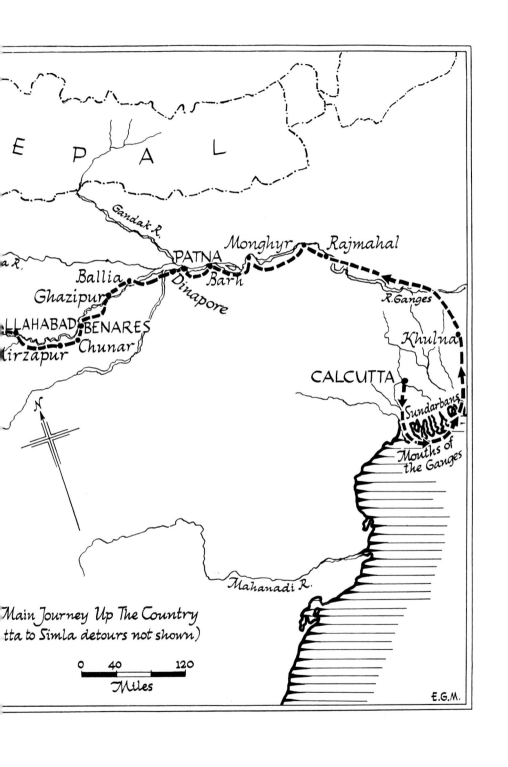

N

Ngandak R.

E P A L

Gandak R.

a R.

Monghyr   Rajmahal

PATNA

Ballia   Barh

Ghazipur   Dinapore

R.Ganges

LLAHABAD BENARES

irzapur   Chunar

Khulna

CALCUTTA

Sundarbans

Mouths of
the Ganges

Mahanadi R.

Main Journey Up The Country
(tta to Simla detours not shown)

0   40   120

Miles

E.G.M.

Introduction

In February 1837. Fanny Eden set out, with her nephew William Osborne, on a tiger-shooting trip to the Rajmahal Hills, 150 miles north-west of Calcutta. This expedition was a modest affair of 260 camp followers and 20 elephants, compared to the cavalcade of 12,000 which accompanied her brother Lord Auckland, Governor-General of India, on his visit to the ruler of the Sikhs, Ranjit Singh, later that year. Fanny and her sister Emily travelled with their brother in great state – and considerable discomfort.

Emily Eden wrote an account of this journey to the Punjab called *Up the Country*, first published in 1866, often reprinted and long one of the classic books of British India. What went unremarked until about thirty-five years ago was that Fanny also recorded this and her earlier hunting trip in illustrated journals. Fanny was as witty, observant and detached a writer as her elder sister and her journals are a highly individual account. When I published extracts from them in my book *The Golden Interlude* in 1955, *The Times* commented, 'One only wishes she had given us more of Fanny's magnificent journals'. The wish is now granted and they are published here complete for the first time.

Fanny Eden was born in Old Palace Yard, Westminster, in 1801, the eighth daughter of William, 1st Baron Auckland, and youngest child of this family of fourteen children. Their father was a son of Sir Robert Eden, of West Auckland, in Co. Durham; their mother, Eleanor Elliot, a sister of the first Earl of Minto, himself a Governor-General of India. Both parents were people of outstanding personality. William Eden held diplomatic posts in America and Ireland, was Minister-Plenipotentiary to the Court of Versailles before the Revolution, and later Ambassador to Spain and to Holland. Mrs Eden accompanied her husband to all his foreign posts, and several of her children were born abroad. It was said that she made domestic life quite fashionable, in an age when children were left almost entirely to the care of nurses and servants.

1

Fanny and her elder sister Emily (born 1797), like their sisters before them, were taught by their mother and by governesses. They had an excellent education. Besides formal lessons, they were encouraged to read anything they wished. They were taken to the play, and taught to have an intelligent interest in foreign affairs. By the time Emily was eighteen and Fanny fourteen, Lady Auckland (as she had now become) had replaced the governesss by a tutor, who had charge of the education of Robert, the brother who came between them in age.

The Edens lived at Eden Farm, the house near Beckenham, in Kent, where their parents had settled after the years abroad. In 1814 Lord Auckland died, so George, the eldest son, succeeded to the title, and began to take his political career seriously. Lady Auckland did not long survive her husband; she died four years after him. She was nicknamed the Judicious Hooker because of her success in marrying off six daughters. Fanny and Emily, the only unmarried daughters, were faced with the decision of what to do about the future. It was not a difficult decision; the answer was inevitable. They would go and live with George. George had to be in London a good deal, and he could not afford to keep up an establishment in town and a house in the country; he and his sisters had each only a limited income. He let Eden Farm to a rich Kentish widow who agreed to take it on his own terms: a seven-year lease at £600 a year. That, George reckoned, would give them the prospect of being settled and comfortable.

The next step was to find a house in London for the three of them. After looking at several, they found one which they liked in Grosvenor Street. Living in London had its compensations, in spite of the lack of a garden. Emily entertained for George, and she and Fanny were entertained in turn by the best Whig society. Emily shone in that milieu; she could argue about politics with men of the first ability and hold her own. Fanny was more detached than her sister about politics, and was apt to smile when the conversation grew too warm. It was useless to argue with Emily about arguing, so Fanny talked about dancing, and bonnets, and gowns, and the latest babies in the family. When she went away on her country-house visits, she wrote long letters to her sister; merry, bubbling letters which always made Emily miss her. Fanny might be regrettably like quicksilver at home, but when she was not there – well, one was very conscious that she was not there. When Emily was away visiting, she was equally aware of there being no Fanny at hand, and was soon mending a pen to write to her younger sister. The only time she did not miss Fanny was when she herself was away with George. Then she did not miss anybody. George's company had always been sufficient in itself.

One of the advantages of living in London was the ease with which they could get away from it. There were many invitations to the country; to stay with the Lansdownes at Bowood, or the Baths at Longleat, or – more unwillingly – the Duke of Devonshire at Chatsworth. Mere magnificence never impressed either Emily or Fanny; they valued character, good humour and good heart above everything else. They liked the Duke of Devonshire, but they did not at all care for the way he took pleasure in making his guests do what they didn't want to do.

Emily enjoyed the friendship of many prominent men, and rumour had from time to time matched her with several of them – even with Lord Melbourne, after the death of his wife, Caroline Lamb. But Emily laughed rumour away each time. Rumour had also been busy with Fanny. A friend wrote to Emily in 1821: 'Does Fanny still keep up "brother and sister" with Edward Drummond? I don't think even Fanny could do it . . .' Edward Drummond was Private Secretary to Sir Robert Peel. Fanny was apparently quite able to keep up 'brother and sister' with him, for she never showed any sign of deeper affection.

As George's career prospered, Fanny's and Emily's life began to lose its tranquillity. In 1830 (like his father) he became President of the Board of Trade and therefore a member of Lord Grey's cabinet. In 1834 Lord Melbourne made him First Lord of the Admiralty. Their duties as hostesses for their brother in London were as nothing, however, compared with their future once he was appointed Governor-General of India in 1835. It was never in doubt that they would accompany him. The Governor-General's party set off for India in the autumn of 1835, intending to make a short stay in Madeira and Rio de Janeiro, that being the usual route, via South Africa, to Calcutta. Neither Fanny nor Emily had ever been to sea before and they found it a devastating experience. After Capetown they also began to realise what the heat of India would be like. It was, in fact, much worse than they had anticipated, but it had to be endured. They would spend their time between Government House in Calcutta and Barrackpore House, which was more pleasant, being fourteen miles up the Hoogly River, and surrounded by gardens. They were thankful when the five months' journey came to an end in February 1836.

There followed many weeks of official entertaining. They were cultivated women, used to entertaining, and they were both naturally friendly, but they soon found that their official position and the second-rate provincialism of Calcutta made it impossible for any real friendships to be formed. Official entertaining meant shaking hands and making conversation with scores of officials while their wives stared at their gowns. There were interminable dinner parties, the guests being scrutinised in advance by Mr Macnaghten and Major Byrne, the Governor-General's Political Secretaries in charge of protocol. It was all very tiring and dull.

Fanny noted everything down in her letters to her closest friend Eleanor Grosvenor. She could forget the tedium and the incessant chatter of people competing for the special attention of the Governor-General's sisters; it was a relief to sit in her own room under a punkah, writing to Eleanor. Her pen glanced and sparkled, lightly skimming the boredom, the clammy heat which descended all too soon, the sense of solitariness which sometimes came upon her.

By the beginning of 1837 the frustrations of this way of life had combined with the stifling climate to affect Fanny's health. Then her nephew William Osborne suggested coming with him tiger shooting. He had served in India before with his regiment, the 16th Lancers and now, aged 30, he was Military Secretary to his Uncle George. Fanny's sense of adventure and acceptance of the odd, unexpected happenings in life meant she was delighted by the prospect. As Emily said, Fanny was 'one of the people who cannot exist without constant excitement.'

Fanny's response to India was a more positive one than Emily's. Emily was prepared to put up with it for the sake of George, to whom she was undoubtedly closer than to her sister. Fanny, though just as subject to homesickness, knew that for her the remedy was plenty of activity and new experiences: 'There are moments when a feeling of desperation comes over me to think that I must dream this dream so distinct from all my past life, for five years. But I mean to make the most of it.'

Emily in *Up The Country* reveals herself as witty, observant and opinionated. Fanny is if anything wittier, more perceptive and shrewd in her observation, and her writing is full of immediacy and élan. Here is all that self-confident vitality and sense of style that came from an assured position among 'The Grand Whiggery', what has been called 'the most agreeable society England has ever known'. Hers is still a thoroughly un-Victorian approach, that of an Austenesque lady, 'strolling about on an elephant', as she puts it, and quizzing India with tolerance and irony. She places no great valuation on her fellow countrymen and their role in the whole performance. There is none of the earnestness and arrogance that soon came in, as the Victorians convinced themselves of their destiny and duty to rule.

First Journal

The Trip to
the Rajmahal Hills

[Emily Eden wrote to a friend in England on December 29th, 1836]

. . . Mrs Bramley has a sharp little sister, a Mrs Cockerell, here, almost pretty and very ill-natured, at least so they say, but we have not found her so the little we have seen of her. She and her husband are going tiger-shooting to the Rajmahal hills. "Cock Robin" and "Jenny Wren," as the little Cockerell couple are familiarly termed, make one of these excursions every year, and Fanny and William mean to join the party, with two or three others. It will be a very good change of scene for her, and something out of the common course of life. Travelling in the marching fashion, which is the way they mean to go, is slow but amusing for a little while. Two sets of tents, one to live in on Monday, while the other is carried on twelve miles, so as to be ready on Tuesday. Everybody in India has their own set of servants, who are no more trouble travelling than living at home. They find their own way from station to station, cook for themselves, sleep on the ground, and, in short, are quite unlike the fussy lady's maid and valet who dispute every inch of the imperial and expect tea, beer, feather beds, etc., at every bad inn on the road. But then, to be sure, it takes about fourteen natives to do the work of one English servant. I suppose William and Fanny could not march without thirty servants of their own, besides guards, elephants, etc. All these, they say, make excellent sketching . . .

Calcutta, January 1837

Fanny to Eleanor Grosvenor

My dear, here is such a plan, such a sublime plan burst upon me! It will eventually conduct me to the bottom of a tiger's throat or the top of a rhinoceros' horn. They do say – it is hardly possible to believe them – that there are *hills* in Bengal, not more than 140 miles from here; and the unsophisticated population of those hills is entirely composed of tigers, rhinoceroses, wild buffalos, and, now and then, a herd of wild hogs. There, I'm going to live for three weeks in a tent. I shall travel the first fifty miles in a palankeen, and then I shall march. It takes a full week to travel a hundred miles in that manner, as our beds, armchairs, tables and clothes all travel on the heads of human beings.

William won't hear reason as to the horrible dangers he is going to take me into. The other two ladies* regularly get upon their elephants and go tiger-hunting every day; they talk of the excitement of the tiger's spring, and the excellent day it was when they saw eight killed. I happen to be very much afraid of a cat – I may say, a kitten. If I were to stay at home while the others were out, a stray tiger would just walk in and carry me off. As George encouragingly observed this morning, 'I see him moving at a round trot with you in his mouth, like a goose over a fox's back.'

[It was going to be a nice little march, William observed to Fanny. No fuss or trouble at all. He had written already for elephants, and they need only have a guard of twenty men. Fanny had better take Jones, in case she should be ill, and the ayah, Myra, to be a companion for the English maid. Then, with Fanny's own sixteen bearers, she would only want ten or twelve more to carry her things. Of course, her kitmutgar would have to go, too, to wait on her at dinner, and peons to pitch her tent, and her jemadar to look after them all, and the washerman and tailor. Those few, with his own tail of servants, would do very well. Fanny ventured to suggest that she was not likely to want any clothes made for the three or four weeks they expected to be away. 'Oh, but tailors are always of use', said William. 'I remember the time a tiger fastened on my elephant's trunk, and so nearly clawed me out of the howdah. My tailor saved the elephant's life by sewing up the wound'. The Journal proper now begins.]

February 13th 1837. Barrackpore.
I am going to try, my dear, if for once in my life, I can keep a journal, and if I can, instead of sending you a doubled up letter I shall send you this book, with an account of our Rajmahal expedition. Such a disturbing event for you, but then you know you can give it to your children for a lesson book on the principle of always making children read for instruction, what everybody else finds too dull to undertake. If I find anything worth sketching I mean to do a sketch, not that I shall make much of that. William and I are here because it is fifteen miles on our road† – that is a march and a half. Do you think we shall get safely back

* In the event, only Mrs Cockerell went, and not Mrs Colvin.   † from Calcutta

again? I have my doubts because the wild beasts in this country are real wild beasts who will not listen to reason. We shall set off after dinner today, so goodbye and God bless you, dear. I have not been very well lately and this journey is to make me strong again.

February 14th. Bullea.
We left Barrackpore at four o'clock yesterday afternoon, went in the carriage to Pultah Ghaut and there left our state behind us in the shape of guards and postillions, and squatted down under the straw covering over a country boat, touching moment of abdicated grandeur. On the other side of the Hoogly we found our palanquins. I had never been in one, and as I first got into mine, felt very much as if I was getting into my coffin. However there was a comfortable bed made up in it. The afternoon was beautiful, not the least hot. William and I were carried along side by side with the doors of our palanquins open, and it was a much more cheerful, and much less shaking form of conveyance than I had expected. When the sun set, though it was bright moonlight, the bearers who ran by the side lighted great torches and we got on quickly, every now and then having to get into a boat to cross some small river.

William had composed himself to sleep just as we reached our encampment, and we trotted past the tents which were a little way off the road. I saw all the servants in full chase after us and at last made them understand that they must stop and the Sahib be woken.

We arrived at seven in the morning, having travelled at the rate of five miles an hour, which is fast for dak travelling. The tents are very comfortable. We find we have 260 people altogether in the camp – half our followers bring their followers. We have twenty elephants, too. Jones, my English maid, travelled in a palanquin with us. Myra, the ayah, I found in a violent fit of anger because we were later than she expected, and she thought we must all have been drowned crossing a river.

I was lying comfortably on a sofa when they ran in to tell William there was a large aligator on the bank of a jeel close by the tent. He took his gun and I went with him, and he shot it so as to wound it, and then it took to the water. Upon which two of the elephants were sent to hunt it there, and it was very grand to see how eager they were and to hear them scream whenever they found it. The chase lasted more than an hour, the elephants trying to trample down the aligator and the aligator turning on them, till at last the mahouts threw themselves off into the water and there were men, elephants and aligator all splashing about together. Then it was driven ashore and William shot it – such an enormous beast.

9

February 15th. Birhampore.
We left Bullea at seven this morning. The vultures and jackals had left nothing but the bones of the aligator.

This is the order of our march. William and I have each a double set of tents and one for our drawing and dining room. There are besides sepoys' tents, cooking tents and a tent for the servants. Jones sleeps in my tent and Myra and Sorga [a maid] in the verandah which goes round it. At night we put all our goods and chattels outside under charge of the sentry. All the inferior servants sleep under trees or make themselves little straw huts.

After dinner we send on our dining tent and two of our sleeping tents, our cooks, baker and half the servants, and we find breakfast ready and tents pitched when we arrive the next morning at the new encamping ground. William and I set off in his tilbury. In case the road should be too bad, we have an elephant stationed half way. Jones and Myra put up my dressing things, and then mount their elephant, and my two jemadars get upon another. The rest of the people follow as they can; palanquins, elephants, hackeries, all appear in the course of two or three hours.

We are encamped today after a march of ten miles under a very thick tuft of trees. The weather is beautiful – really cold till twelve o'clock, and there is the sound of birds all round us, and the sun so well shut out we are able to sit outside our tents. There is a large elephant bored with the flies, and he has picked a large bough for himself and brushes them off with the greatest ease. Spring has begun now and the jungles look beautiful with the different shades of green and the red cotton tree. It has no leaves yet, only large crimson flowers, like a daphne multiplied the size of an elm.

The Musselman jemadar Ariffe (you must learn to know their names) brought in a handful of wild ducks he had shot, which he handsomely offered us for dinner and we as handsomely declined. That pompous old bore Dulhoo condescendingly accepted the same, though he could not eat anything religiously which had died such a death by a Musselman's hand. Ariffe cut all their throats after they were dead, so satisfying his conscience and his hunger without inflicting any great pain upon the dead ducks. At four o'clock William took his gun and I my sketch book and got upon our elephant and went out after subjects. I found the little temple and made a masterly sketch of it for you from the top of the elephant, while William went from one Jeel to another, murdering the innocent wild ducks. If he goes out of sight for five minutes I begin to think it very shocking to be left alone in the middle of Asia.

February 16th. Pangotta.
We did not set off till half past 7 this morning for a march of six miles. The country perfectly hideous, flat uncultivated plain, nothing uneven but the road. However, we contrived to extricate ourselves from the ruts. We came the whole way in the tilbury and there was a great improvement the last mile. We passed a river and a really pretty village, the huts with verandahs neatly thatched and great signs of farming implements about. The instant we come in sight the women cover up their faces and scuttle away as fast as they can. One of them, having no other means of escape, scrambled over a high mud wall with her child sitting on her hip, the way they always carry children here. There was a native come out to look at us in such a shawl. No, I never saw such a tempting article! I would have offered an elephant for it, only I thought William would make some foolish objection. The man in rank must have been a pendant to our English farmers. The shawl must have been very remarkable for the instant Jones arrived she said, 'Ma'am, did you see *that* man in *that* shawl?' We had passed a great many other men in a great many other shawls. She sighed and said, 'What a pity to let him keep it', and I sighed and agreed. The weather is quite perfect, no fog, no dew, and the temperature is seventy at the

11

hottest time of the day. I feel exactly twice as strong as I did four days ago in Calcutta.

William is out shooting snipes and I have got up a case of oppression for him when he comes home. Ariffe, who speaks excellent English, has been telling me that some of the villagers have been following him from the last station to complain that the elephant jemadar and the sepoy havildar and my kitmutgar who caters for us, took their fish, kids and eggs without paying for them, and beat one old man who had a natural distaste for parting with his property on those terms. I hear a great deal of loud recrimination going on, and I suspect from the looks of the culprits that we recently performed the guilty act of eating a stolen dinner.

William has just come home with some snipes and quails, so we shall have something to eat which has been honestly earned today – and we have had a regular trial: Ariffe and the villagers on one side, and the culprits on the other, who had nothing to say for themselves. So now we are to send on every day to the Thanadar, the head of the village, to tell him not to let anybody have anything till it is paid for. As this constant change of air makes one very hungry I shall go with my own little purse and buy our own little dinner.

February 17th. Dupore.
We had a long march this morning, twelve miles. I do not like our encamping ground – it is in the middle of a village, and I expect the Pariah dogs to eat us up in the night, or the dacoits to carry off ourselves as we leave nothing else for them in the tents. Will it shock you to know that though exceptionally like gypsies in other respects, we have something bordering on civilization in our tents in the shape of a chess board and cards, and play – at chess for an hour after luncheon while William smokes his hookah and when it is too glaring to look out even; and at cards for half an hour after dinner because I am too tired to go out then, and from some cause which nobody has yet explained it is utterly impossible to see to read or write in India by candlelight with any comfort.

We are engaged in a very complicated system of gambling, and the grand result is to be a large ivory elephant which we are to have manufactured at Morshadabad, *the* place for ivory carvings. It will simply be the death of me if William should win it. We met a messenger from Mr Melville this morning – he is the political agent and we shall sleep at his house at Barhampore tomorrow night. Mr Forbes the Magistrate has sent us a large escort of people with swords and spears. I hope they are not the Nawaub of Morshadabad's troops in disguise come to take us prisoners.

12

Sunday February 18th. Barhampore.

We are in a house again and have a solid roof over our heads and pucker walls round us. All people here say a pucker house meaning a brick house, and as it makes me uncomfortable to hear them I will try the same trick upon you. A house is clearly a very inferior habitation to a tent – a very confined feel about it, and mosquitos in full flight. We have not had one in our tents. However, we are very comfortable here. Mr Melville, for which I owe him gratitude, had paved the way for my being too tired to receive visits or sit through a great dinner, so we took a drive to that great banyan tree, which I fancy that pen-and-ink sketch makes you see just as distinctly as if you had been there. Moreover, on the other end of the wall, actually in the trunk of the tree, there is a temple with a monster of an idol in it – opposite the idol there is another building with two long iron prongs coming up, and between the prongs the victims that are sacrificed are placed. There were very apparent marks that victims had been there, and though they talked of animals I was not to be taken in because I heard such a shocking true story yesterday of a temple near at hand, where it has just been dis-covered that they are in the habit on one particular festival of impaling a man and, when he is impaled and before he is dead, they take pincers and tear him, as if he were a second Damiens.*

I went to the chapel this morning where Mr Hill, a Missionary, preached and there was the Presbyterian service. It was a very striking sermon, violently Methodistical with anecdotes of different individuals eloquently told. He preaches twice a day in the bazaars to the natives. The Europeans at the station are very fond of him, they say he is a sincere religious enthusiast. Mr Forbes and a Mr and Mrs Rishel dined with us. The poor woman is just arrived, half broken hearted at leaving four children at home under the care of strangers. She was to have left the fifth but when the ship was at the point of sailing she could not part with it and smuggled it aboard.

19th February. Morshadabad.

We came on here yesterday afternoon. It was a very pretty eight miles drive and Mr Melville brought us in his carriage. From some dim recol-lection I have of the state of my own mind when I was in England I can just fancy, dearest, that you may not be intimately acquainted with the public and private history of the Nawaub of Morshadabad. Indeed, I should not very much wonder if you are at this moment carrying on life

* The unsuccessful assassin of Louis XV, tortured in this way before being torn to
  pieces by four horses.

at Motcombe* without any inconvenient recollection of his existence. This Nawaub borders too much upon what we call here for want of anything better the political affairs of the country, for me to venture to ask many questions about him, but as far as I can make out from my own accurate observation, he is one of the native princes living under our tender care and protection. The city of Morshadabad and [?£]70,000 a year we leave him in possession of, with Mr Melville settled close at hand to watch him and how he spends his income. Mr Melville has arranged to spend a considerable portion of it for him, very much against his own consent, because we say he is a dissipated young man and would waste it if left to himself. So we have been building a palace for him, a magnificent modern looking palace which would make our King's new palace turn pale with envy. A Colonel Macleod planned it and has superintended the building. A thousand workmen have been employed upon it for six years. One more year will see it finished, and of all the palaces I have seen it strikes me as one of the most perfect, so beautiful outside and such splendid rooms within, all to be paved with grey marble from China. The dining room and the ballroom are two of the handsomest I ever saw, each 170 feet long. The immense heights of rooms here add so much to their beauty. They have brought out mirrors and large panes of glass for it from England, and 800 panes of glass were broken in the course of the voyage. £60,000 will pay the whole cost of the building.

The Nawaub till last week never entered the doors but stuck to his determination that he did not want a new palace and would rather not live in it. Last week he softened on the subject and went over it and was delighted. He is to furnish it himself – it is to be hoped he will manage better than the R. of Lucknow, who brought over some fine statues and set them up standing on their heads.

He sent us many civil messages, wished to come out to meet us, which would have puzzled me considerably. He sent word that he would let us encamp in the town instead of outside it – it was the greatest favour he could do. Accordingly we are encamped in the court of the palace, which is against his rule, but there is much to see here, and we have only a day or two to see it, so it is a great convenience to be in the heart of the city, which extends for eight miles.

You would have laughed at our arrival. Mr Melville and Mr Forbes make us be followed about this district by a large retinue of silver sticks. There was an enormous crowd of natives waiting to see us before we went into our tents. I got into a tonjaun. William, Mr Melville and Mr Forbes walked by it around the outside of the palace, all the natives

* The Grosvenors' country seat

14

following, and the chief architect who happily spoke English, coming to be complimented, attention all the time fixed on his magnificent white shawl. We have been dining at Mr Cunningham's, a son of Alan Cunningham's and a brother of our A de C. He is the only European Resident here and has a very pretty bungalow by the side of the river.

February 20th

We went this morning to see some beautiful mosques. There are no end to them in the city. I sketched too an old gun which a fig tree has grown into. Nobody knows how it got there. The Nawaub sent us a great quantity of fish, vegetables and fruit in baskets covered with scarlet cloth, and later in the day so did the old Begum. Her fish were very far from fresh but the servants were happy to eat it all. I was to have visited the Begum but she was sick and I was tired, so we put it off till we return. We have been ordering some things from a very clever ivory carver. Have had more fish from a deputation of fisherwomen who insisted on seeing us because they always see the Lord Sahib, who we modestly suggested we were not.

February 21st. [illegible]

We had a short march here of eight miles, the first three through the city on an elephant. We passed a beautiful temple with a rival clay elephant as the idol, and upon the whole, though I condescended to sketch the other, we on our own elephant looked the most worshipful of the two.

Morshadabad must have been a splendid city in its day, the riverside seemed as we passed to be bordered by mosques. The market place was a beautiful sight, four old gateways lead into it – a mosque in good preservation is seen through them. The swarms of natives buying and selling seemed without end. Did you ever study the *Arabian Nights* enough to remember the kabobs of Beirut selling in the market place? They were serving up these on skewers. The bazaar round looked quite brilliant from their manufacture of silver fringes and shoes, that sort of convenient shape they make them . . .

We had deep shade for the rest of our drive, the cotton trees and bamboos almost meeting over our heads, and now we are encamped in a jungle, which is always satisfactory. The tents are in shade all day, and no glare. The weather is quite perfect, no fogs or dew as there are at Calcutta, the thermometer at the hottest time of the day seldom above seventy-six in the tents.

15

This looks to me like a flourishing place for rising young tigers and we are going out in the afternoon as usual after game and sketches, like two babes in the wood on an elephant. There's a pleasing sound of singing birds here today such as I never heard at Calcutta. I do not like the notion of going back to that great hot shut-up prison of a palace.

Now we are in a scrape. We thought we were within twenty-six miles of the place of meeting and have just got a message to tell us that there has been a mistake about it and that the rest of the party will be encamped at Oudinella fifty-six miles on, and we were all to have met on the 23rd and plunge deep into the jungles on the 24th. Ten miles is the right length for a march, and if we go much more all the bearers who carry the furniture begin to grumble. Still, if we are more than one day behind the rest we shall throw out all their arrangements if they wait for us, or lose them altogether if they do not. So, dear, what would you advise us to do? We have just seen the elephant Jemadar who says he will contrive for us to go seventeen miles tomorrow, and William has stopped a country cart for me to sketch and means to have one like it for the course at Calcutta [see above].

February 22nd. Comra.
Here's a heartrending situation. After seven miles on an elephant, six in the tilbury on a road which made our progress very much like sailing in a

16

ship in a short sea, within five miles of the place of encampment, we passed first five men with our breakfast and dining table on their heads, two more with my sofa, two more with chairs, and in the distance the distracting sight of Sepoys guarding hackeries, the carts that carry our kitchen utensils, they being drawn by bullocks, advancing at the rate of 1½ miles per hour.

Our fates flashed upon us at once. These were our advanced supplies. We were to find nothing but empty tents. No breakfast, nothing, and so it is. We set off at six and now it is nine, and for three hours we have no chance of anything, our tents upon a great arid plain with nothing to be seen but Sepoys and tent-pitchers cooking their dinners which they would probably throw away if I contaminated their eatables by looking at them. It shows great mental energy that I should be writing this to you with a pencil, and have sketched mortals who have food to put in their mouths. William is smoking a cigar in a state of placid contentment that is very irritating to see, and what is more he has got hold of the Thanadar and together they are going to empty the village of its innocent and simple inhabitants and hackeries, that they may relieve our own servants tomorrow and enable us to push on twenty miles.

Of course we must mean to take our kitchen utensils in the tilbury – he won't get me to lose sight of them again in a hurry. The baker, evidently a most exemplary man, has in a most supernatural manner produced some gingerbread nuts, everybody else in the camp having denied the possibility of getting a bit of bread.

It is half-past-twelve and we have breakfasted. Our breakfast was enlivened by old Dulhoo bursting in in a fury such as I never saw equalled by any man, but probably soon shall by a tiger. His gesticulations were so vehement I expected his dagger would have been through us both, and his utterances so rapid, I could not understand one word of what he was saying. The whole storm burst upon William, who finds the government of a camp no sinecure.

At last it appeared that a monster whom we have seen wandering about the camp with, I might say, a remarkable absence of clothing, is Dulhoo's servant and cooks his dinner; that he had desired the said monster should travel on an elephant with Ariffe and some of our servants. They had arrived without him and he suspected that they had turned him off. All the others being Musselmen, cook for each other, but he being a Hindu must have a Hindu to cook for him. William humbly represented that all his servants walked and that Dulhoo's servant would not cook the worse for walking too. But he was in much too great a fury to listen, and we still heard him roving about the camp scolding whoever came near him.

17

February 23rd

We accomplished our twenty miles with great success this evening, and got in to the tilbury on the side of the river which the elephants had to swim. We saw some unhappy dak travellers sitting under a tree by their palanquin without any bearers to carry them on. It is sometimes necessary here to arrange ten days beforehand the relays of bearers that are wanted. If they choose to set the traveller down in the middle of a jungle he has no redress. When we got up we found the victims were Mr and Mrs Cockerell, the heads of the party we are going to join, a remarkably small couple with a remarkably small lapdog, and there they all sate in apparently a state of placid contentment, he with a book in his hand and she holding an umbrella over her head, and nothing in the shape of a human habitation near. Our natural questions were, 'Where are your bearers?' 'Oh, . . . abroad over the country, I believe. If you happen to meet any, send them on to us.' We suggested their mounting the first of our elephants that should pass, and coming on to our camp, but they did not dare leave their palanquins. Happily before we were four miles from them we met a set of bearers in full trot towards them. Some other travellers had taken them on and they were like tired post horses.

We are encamped in a beautiful bit of jungle, such fine trees, the ground tumbled, and high fern. Our elephants are all tired, so we are obliged to confine ourselves to the inward economy of our camp. I have been to see the elephants' supper cooked. A great deal more trouble is taken with it than with our dinners. The Nawaub has lent William two hunting elephants, so now we have twenty-two, and his ones treated very royally, their cakes made up in a mould and their wine better than some of the vin ordinaire. Then we went to see our advance stores set off, and an absurd sight it was, some of the men in red blankets, some in shawls, some I may say in no clothing at all, the elephants kneeling to be loaded, the wretched bullocks having their hackeries stuffed full of the property of every servant in the camp who ought to carry it themselves. I sketched two men who were half an hour packing up the kedgeree pot which holds the store of water for the camp, Ariffe rating them all the time. Dulhoo bored one of the villagers so much, he fairly dropped his load and ran away.

February 24th. Oudenella.

There we are, dear, in the very jaws of the tigers. The first man we asked about them said that he had heard one roar at twelve o'clock last night, an hour that makes it peculiarly awful. There are hills all round and

about us and a beautiful old bridge opposite our tents [see p. 5]. The rest of the party's tents are on the other side of it. Besides the Cockerells there are only Mr Stopford, a cousin of Lord Stopford, Mr Holroyd, a relation of the Fanes, and a Mr Bracken who once had his foot in a tiger's mouth, and has been an amateur tiger hunter ever since. We have seen none of them yet – they went out hunting at four this morning, that wonderful little woman Mrs Cockerell with them, and they are only now reported as arriving home.

We have just seen them. They have found no tigers but have brought home quantities of spotted deer and black partridges – the sort of savage animals I should prefer meeting. Mrs C. has actually been thirty miles on an elephant during the hottest hours of the day. Ten miles knocks me up, and if I am out in the sun after two o'clock I come home with my head splitting, and hardly a woman ventures out later. In the morning the wind was really cold. We had our first sight of the Ganges, which looks more like a small lake than a river. In the middle of the day the sun was burning hot, thermometer 89 in the tents, and the hunting people had been through a change of more than 45 degrees in twelve hours. Tomorrow morning they are going on what they call a home beat over some very pretty hilly jungles. I shall go with them for a little while.

February 25th

I got up at six, put myself in Mrs C's howdah, and made my elephant follow that I might come home when I pleased. Jones and Ariffe were on their two ponies . . . The jungles are beautiful at this time of the year, every tree covered with blossoms of different colours, and creepers which would make . . . stare; the peacocks flying in every direction; their screams have a sound of home; herds of spotted deer starting out at every step, and then the quantity of elephants beating about, and the line of shooters on theirs which are as eager as this one.

While I was with them we saw nothing worse than wild hogs, but I had not left them less than ten minutes before they found a tiger and wounded him, but instead of showing fight he ran away as fast as he could. One rhinocerous has appeared in the distance and when he does charge an elephant it is tremendous.

I set off to go home through the jungle we had beat with nobody to defend me against tigers if they should come but Ariffe and his dagger, and nothing to offer them to eat but Jones, when the elephant suddenly stopped, threw up his trunk and began to scream. If there had been any use in it I should have begun to scream, too, and they say he actually must have smelled a tiger, so I must not try the trick of coming home again alone. But the real fact is I fear the sun the most of the two. I am low about seeing no monkeys.

20

February 26th. Rajmahal.

We moved six miles today and all the way through jungles literally over-run with wild roses covered with blossoms. The gentlemen have with them each six rifles in their howdahs and shoot at all the innocent wild beasts they meet. Just as I was disserting upon the exceeding beauty of one rose bush, a great wild hog rushed out of it and charged the elephant Mrs C. and I were upon. The instant after, it had five balls through it and then, dear, I settled that I had no taste for the shooting part of the expedi-tion, and shall confine my ideas to the picturesque, and there is more than enough to spare of it here. I thought that hog's was a shocking case of murder, not that I looked at it, but from what I gathered from all they were saying about it the elephants set to work to trample it to death, and when at last it was dead and they insisted upon my looking at it, it seemed to be such a fine strong beast so exactly fitted to its own jungles – I do not see our right to take our love of destruction there.

We found our tents pitched in the midst of fine old ruins. Such sketching, if the sun would not shine so brightly and make it impossible to look out of the tent.

I am in a dreadful state of puzzle. I heard going round the breakfast table this morning: 'To be sure, how strange that we should be eating our breakfast *here*, in a tent, when we think what it was,' and if I were to think for ever I should only think how strange it would be if we were not eating our breakfast, when we have been up and shaken upon our elephants for the last three hours. If I am right it must be by inspiration, but I have a sort of idea that these are the ruins of the palace that once belonged to the King of Burdwan, and I daresay it is owing to some horrible atrocity of ours that it is not a very good palace still. If any of our party have a fault, they are rather long about what we used to call in the nursery our 'meals', and I sketched my tent and the little bit of ruin behind it surreptitiously while they were finishing. Then – you see that gateway – William handsomely went out with me this afternoon sketch-hunting instead of tiger-hunting, and you see what a treasure of a place it is and how happy he looks [see p. 22]. You cannot see that because I was obliged to fetch out my large sketchbook, but we did find in the middle of the jungle a sort of lawn sur-rounded by palm trees and ruins, and with our elephants feeding in the middle, that was too perfect. I write pompously about my sketches because I happen not to be able to sketch at all, only have a sort of King of Burdwan's inspiration for present use.

The villagers here are nice looking people. The Ganges is on one side of us, looking like a smooth blue sea. The Hoogly is a very inferior article and the poor dear Thames a miserable stream, not to be named with either. That last sentence is what I call real Indian patriotism.

February 27th

The rest of the party have crossed to an island to shoot. I was afraid of being kept out in the sun and so got on my elephant and came seven miles to a new encampment, and anything more thoroughly eastern or prettier than the country we passed through it is impossible to conceive. For the first two miles we passed through the straggling remains of the city, very grand remains of old buildings – then we came to the Ganges on one side and high hilly jungle on the other, one mass of different colours with the blossoms and magnificent palm trees and bamboos rising from it – besides the red cotton tree there is a sort of coral-looking tree which is too beautiful, and these again are festooned by creepers

22

quite endless in variety, and rose trees with white roses growing higher than our heads.

Soon we got into the thick of the jungle, where there is only room for an elephant to pass, and we came to an old mosque which seems to be quite inaccessible, the trees and arches have grown together. It was too nearly over my head for me to try to draw it but I sketched two others on the road. There are hundreds of peacocks flying in these jungles – their scream sounds real and familiar and gives me an idea that I am not dreaming all this, which if I am left alone for five minutes and look round I am tempted to think I am.

The first sight of our encampment was most satisfactory: a temple standing on a rock and our tents among trees at the bottom of it, with the Ganges rolling past. They are just come home from their expedition, having done nothing in the way of tigers. It is very pretty to see thirty elephants swimming the rivers with their drivers standing on their heads. In the afternoon I set off with an elephant and a tonjon to try to get up to the top of the rock, but the path was so steep and stony, neither the elephants nor bearers could get on; so I continued to walk up the rest of the way taking a large escort with me for fear of a stray tiger. The view was beautiful and there was a horrid great idol that the brahmins let me look at without going into the temple and they even let me sit down on the step to draw. The Musselmen servants took off their shoes and went in to salaam to the idol.

February 28th. Rajmahal Hills.
Once more here's a situation for you to think of. We have moved our tents five miles, the others are shooting their way here and will probably go twenty. Their tents have not come up for they have not a double set, but I was so taken by the situation of William's and mine which were by the side of a jeel covered with wildfowl with the whole line of hills in the distance – I desired them to pitch the tent we were to sit in quite at the edge, there being scarcely room for it. Well, there I settled myself to the innocent occupation of writing a letter, when some of the servants ran in and pointed to what I thought an otter swimming, which otter rose out of the water and turned out to be a small part of an alligator's head, the tail being at a considerable distance – so very pleasant, it will be poking in its head in a minute and reading this. I am very fond of alligators – I say this to please it. And in this my utmost need I am deprived of Ariffe, the only man in the camp who could speak English reason to it. I have handsomely lent him to William because he can load a gun.

By way of making me quite comfortable, when I sent for my ayah to

23

Washing the elephants

tell her to stop the men who were in the jeel getting water, as I had a particular dislike to see an alligator eat a man (they are too great fatalists to get out of his way), she answered 'Yes, Ladysheep, plenty aligater, three there'. And there are actually three lying on the opposite bank. Not make-believe beasts at all but eighteen or twenty feet long, and I have nothing but Mrs Cockerell's little lapdog to offer them in exchange for myself. These men will be the death of me, they are all in the water again in spite of all the Kitmutgar can say to prevent them. Now they are putting a trough to stand upon and I am better. They are come back now and twenty-seven elephants have swam the jeel, so that will settle the aligators for the present. They have found no tigers yet. I mean to go a little way with them tomorrow as they will hardly be out of sight of the tents and I can come back when I like.

March 1st
I have been out, dear, from six till half-past-nine and have seen a great deal. We had thirty-two elephants out this morning to beat the jungles and to be sure, they were jungles that required beating. What is called high grass jungles, the grass being the consistency of timber, it seems to me, so very much higher than elephant, howdah and human creature; nothing to be seen of them at five yards distance, nothing heard but the

24

crunshing of the reeds by the elephants as they break their way through, which is hard work for them. Our mahout has orders to keep close to Mr B, who is the guide of the party, for our safety consists in being in the thick of the shooters, who have no time to think about us but would naturally shoot any animal that would attack us because it is the object they are after.

I was glad when we had made our way through that into some soft grass jungle, and very soon the elephant we were on and two others near gave a roar and an immense rhinocerous started up within a yard of us. All those near us shot and all declared it was hit but if it were it bore it very philosophically. While some were chasing that, our elephant still was snorting where we were – and then we found a young rhinocerous was left, not much larger than a great pig. They wanted to take him alive but he shewed much more fight than the mother – charged a line of sixteen elephants and made them roar and turn round, for they hate a small live thing. The mahouts threw themselves off to bind it with cords, but though they caught it three times, at last it fairly got the better of them all and escaped to the thick jungles. Ten minutes later we found another old rhinocerous, probably the respected father – a very magnificent looking beast, and the chase after him was beautiful. All the elephants get so eager and press on as hard as they can. He made his escape too, which I was not as sorry for as I ought to have been, for the half-hour's chase was just as grand to see. After that I left them to come home across what was called a safe bit of country, and in that same bit within a quarter of a mile of the camp they killed their first tiger ten minutes after I left them, and Mrs C. came home smaller and fresher and better dressed than ever, quite delighted and only wishing it had shewn more fight.

March 2nd
We are still in the same place, and they killed two more tigers this morning which shewed more fight than the others. There is some satisfaction in a tiger being killed – the natives crowd round the body and are so pleased. Last night just as I was going to bed they came and told me a rajah had brought me a spotted deer, two peacocks and a pot of honey, and as they were jungle productions I was not to refuse them. I sent my salaam, wondering what on earth I should do with the peacocks, but he made such a point of making his salaam to the 'Lady Sahib' I went out in a pink flannel dressing gown, which I hope he thinks an approved English mode of dress. There he was in a gold kincob* dress and turban with his

* brocade

servants holding torches, and the peacocks and the deer, which turns out the greatest of pets, follows me about and lies by me on the sofa like a little dog.

March 3rd

We are still in the same place. I did not go out with them this morning as it turned out not safe to come home. They had not been gone ten minutes before I heard a great discharge of guns and was sure they had found a tiger. And now they have brought an immense one across an elephant to the door of my tent. All I know about it is that 'Osborne Sahib' shot it. It is an awful looking beast – its skin measures twelve feet from the end of the head to the root of the tail. One comfort is, one stroke from such a claw would not leave one to linger. While I am writing this I cannot but think how intensely tiresome this old tiger-hunting story must be to you to read. They are just coming – the tiger was springing when William disabled it with a shot and he and Mr Bracken killed it.

March 4th

We moved three miles today among some fresh hills, very pretty and thoroughly English and the air feels English too. They found another rhinocerous and shot it. Generally that operation is amusing to the shooters and the rhinocerouses – they almost always get away, and no wonder, for they go at a gallop while the elephants shuffle after them at a quick walk, screaming and throwing up their trunks and making all the fuss they can. I do not know why it is but the instant I am on an elephant I do not feel the least afraid for myself or anybody else. When the tall grass shakes and the elephants begin to scream, I ask whether it is a tiger or a rhinocerous in exactly the same tone I should ask of the servants whether it is a partridge or pheasant. Some of the servants met a tiger this morning, but it walked on never minding. They found then the half-eaten body of a man.

The gentlemen are out again this afternoon. There are some lovely sketches about, but William says it is not safe to go. However, Mrs C. and I went a little way on our elephant, and did nothing more frightful than put up a jungle cat, which is little larger than our cats, but as it bounds through the camp it looks like a little tiger. They all began screaming out 'Tiger', at which Jones and Myra barricaded themselves in my tent. One very clever man called out 'No Tiger', upon which they called louder than ever 'Young Rhinocerous', and Jones and Myra added an extra chair to their barricadoes.

March 5th
We remain here today for they are still after a tiger. Yesterday it was
Sunday and I staid at home thinking I was going to read prayers, but the
Hindoo religion is so much more vociferous than mine. It is one of their
festivals and many hundreds are preparing to wash in a stream near here
and to offer plantains and kids, and what with their screaming and singing and tom-toms and the bleating of the kids, I don't think I ever
heard such a noise before. Of course Dulhoo said he must go, and
instead of offering a kid has brought one back, so have half the servants
in the camp – sacred little kids that are not to be eaten. But it is a dinner
time, and a suspicious lull is come over them.

I went a little way on the elephant this afternoon, and nothing can be
prettier than these hills, the creeper growing over the trees makes their
colouring so beautiful. There was one exactly like an aspen with a view
of a hill and cascade through it, and the creeper one mass of yellow
flowers. When I was lying comfortably on the sofa, a snake riggled from
under William's chair, so unpleasant.

March 6th
We have again moved three miles, still in the hills, and all the way we
came perfectly beautiful, but nothing for the shooters except peacocks,
deer and wild partridges. The elephants pick up the birds that are
killed. I saw Dulhoo rush up to Jones with a stick today when she came

out of my tent, and thought he was gone mad, but there was a large scorpion on her cloak as big as the top of a teacup, which had settled itself there in the night. She had a narrow escape for their sting is horrible, and if it is the same to everybody, I had rather not have scorpions in my tent at night. My little deer is such a treasure – he travels in my howdah and I hope hides his face when they shoot any of his connections. He has his own spoon, teacup and saucer and will not hear of drinking out of anything but his spoon, and is very particular about the grass and young leaves he makes his servant pluck for him, and he trots after me from one tent to another in the most majestic manner.

The hills grow prettier and prettier. My tent is pitched close by the remains of an old bath you see, and the palanquins, and a contemplative native sitting by his hookah. There has been a squall of wind which has filled the tent with dust as far as I can see. William is sitting back in his armchair in the last choking agonies. Two nights ago there was a violent storm. I thought I was to be suffocated in bed, to say nothing of the chances of the tent flying bodily away.

We have changed our route and the consequence is George may be recalled and he and Emily set sail and I not know it, for I shall get no letters for ten days. They have heard of tigers three marches off – 'real good tigers' Mrs C. says, 'worth going after, for I understand they have eaten quantities of human creatures'. William and I strolled about on an elephant this afternoon and beautiful it was, wild rose trees and reed grass on tumbled ground, higher than one's head, and the hills in the distance. All the litter of our camp mixed up with the ruins of small mosques. I sketched one where there is the head of a dead saint and which is inhabited by such a live one. The servants say that two tigers come every day and sweep it clean with their tails.

March 7th
We came eight miles today. I came with the shooters the first five miles and saw them beat through jungles which are evidently chiefly remarkable for the peaceful character of the brute inhabitants. I say nothing, but if I were given to shooting I could shoot deer and peacocks without having fifty elephants to help me. We passed a man lying near a path who looked dead but he was still breathing. His friends had taken all his ornaments and left him there to die, if the jackalls and vultures did not eat him first.

I left the shooters the last three miles and came in the tonjon with an elephant to guard me. I never saw such a wild scene as I passed through nor felt more obliged to the tigers for not appearing. The natives burn the jungles at this time of year and of an evening the flames on the hills are very grand. This morning at one part of the road the jungle was burning at each side and we had to make a detour to get past, the bearers singing a sort of melancholy chorus all the time, 'Jeldu, Jeldu Kubbadar', 'Make haste, make haste, Have a care'. The tall palm trees rising out of the flames and smoke looked like a scene on the stage, but the heat was so great I was glad when we had passed.

I am sure if you could just step over that 15,000 miles of that old horror of a sea, the two months journey we are taking would delight you. In general things seem as if they are more extraordinary than they are when one comes to see them, but it is utterly impossible to make you know how unlike to any life one has ever dreamed of before this tent life is. When we go up the country at the end of the year with all our pomp about us it will not be half as amusing, but if we get back without any calamities from tigers or jungle fevers, this journey will have been a most successful experiment. I have twice the strength I had when I left Calcutta. As to William, if he gets twenty miles deeper in the jungles I do not believe it will be possible for him to be caught up and led back again to his military secretaryship – he will go off as one of the elephants did last night.

March 8th
We have moved seven miles today. They shot deer and partridges all the way. I wrote to you about the Thugs, the people who religiously strangle their fellow creatures. One confessed the other day after a long life of Thugism that he had assisted at the deaths of seven hundred. We passed the remains of an old fort today, and the hills near it are a stronghold of the Thugs. The foot of the precipice I sketched was one of their burial places for their victims. I could only sketch it as the elephants moved on but there were other tempting ruins in sight.

A bullock was eaten by a tiger two nights ago in the village where we are encamped. The gentlemen all went out again this afternoon and saw a very large tiger but in such thick jungle he got away. There is but one step from the jungle to our tents and a jackall just now put his head out within three yards of me, which promises well for the remainder of the night.

March 9th
We are staying on here, excessively baffled by the tigers. They saw a large one yesterday afternoon, but in such thick jungle the elephants

could not make their way after him. However, this morning was to be *the* morning when I was to see a tiger killed – an operation which by great good luck I had as yet escaped. The jungles were close at hand. We took the field in great state with all our elephants – strong in several cheerful incidents – such as one of the elephants' drivers being nearly carried off in the night, only saved by the screaming of his elephant. Before we got fifty yards from the village we found the body of a pony which had been killed and half eaten in the night, and the marks of tigers' feet about it. There was something grand in the way all the elephants set off stamping and screaming and followed up the traces of the tiger in jungles where it seemed 'a sin and a shame' to fancy a tiger could be, soft grass with clumps of rose bushes white with roses and thousands of butterflies fluttering over them – and no tiger ever did appear. Upon the whole I should say we are rather baffled considering we are what they call tiger-hunting, but they must bring down their noble minds to the calibre of deer and black partridges, and to me the beauty of the country and the uncounted quantity of air and liberty we are allowed are much more enjoyable even than I expected it would be.

March 10th

They are not vanquished yet, and again set off to fresh jungles at six this morning. There is William's elephant and his row of beaters waiting for his appearance from his tent, and some have magnificent tusks but very few have any. They are the best beasts to see much of. I cannot say the respect I have for them. Though not naturally witty I suspect they have much more common sense than we have. When the sun is hot they throw dust on their backs if they cannot get grass, and when that gets heated they brush it off with their trunks and throw on fresh.

I went off on a bold expedition of my own this morning. When they set off upon theirs I had a hankering after those Thug ruins which are only three miles off. There is a sort of a semblance of a road to them over the hills where an elephant can go – so arming myself with Jones and Dulhoo, both equally efficient, I suspect, in case of danger, I set off after them trusting to William's assertion that the tigers would not attack an elephant, nor the Thugs strangle a woman. 'Murray' is the Hindustani word for carcase,* and it gives them all the greatest pleasure to find one, because they instantly assume that it must be the remains of a tiger's dinner. By way of making me quite happy William affectionately added, 'I'm sure I shall be very sorry if anything does happen to you, but at the same time it will be a melancholy consolation to find your half-eaten Murray –'.

* See Glossary

We went through an awful pass where the banks were higher than our heads, so if a tiger had sprung it would have sprung into our howdah. That round thatched roof I sketched is what people sleep under to watch their crops – they are safe there from wild beasts of any kind, and I was amused by a hut on the ground, inhabited by a whole family, being so much smaller than a hen-coop – the owner was a wretched cripple half covered over by straw [see p. 32].

Jehagurry – That is part of the fort, a little further on – the view of the valley beneath was lovely, and I even looked with philosophy at the 'Murray' of a buffalo that had not been long killed and four vultures sitting on a tree looking at it. While I was sketching, the Post passed us – the man carrying the letters, who for six shillings a month goes full trot every day twenty-five miles through this tiger country at all hours, with nothing but a large stick to help himself with, and professing his full belief that the tigers eat human creatures by the dozen. I was so proud of not being eaten I went through the gateway and found a remarkably eligible ruin a little farther on, the remains of one old mosque, and moreover a view of our tents from it. They all returned home in a discomfited state, with some innocent peacocks, and we are to move tomorrow.

March 11th

We are in a terrible way today, can find no jungle with beasts of any kind in them – came through six miles of jungle where the elephants could only get on by pulling down trees with their trunks and breaking off branches over our heads. Their strength and cleverness about it were quite wonderful, and so was the beauty of the trees and shrubs, but it was not so pleasant to be crashing through them in that way.

We got to our encampment at half-past-nine and being in this state of destitution settled to march eight miles in the afternoon, and so take us to the banks of the Ganges which we are to cross tomorrow, turn our faces towards Calcutta and shoot our way home. William and I thought as there was no regular road it would be new and clever if we were to go in his tilbury, and so we did, a man running before us with a great stick, as far as we could make out that he might serve as food for any wild beasts that might appear. We did accomplish the drive, but I think we came on one wheel all the way, first one and then the other. Happily the banks each side were too narrow to allow us to be overturned. This is the last day of being among the hills – when we cross the river tomorrow we get back to that horrid plain of Bengal which has nothing but white ants' nests to break it.

March 12th. Pierpointy.

I daresay you have never been sufficiently struck by the delicacy of my conduct in having spared you the names of all the villages we have stopped at in the hills – very bad Indian names – they might have given you a jungle fever. This being the last, I have written it, but it shows the perversity of the country that instead of calling it Pierpoint which any Christian would, they make it ridiculous by turning it into Pierpointy.

I am writing this in the pleasantest of situations, but I was getting uneasy about having no hardships. Now our position is perfectly heart-rending. There are two or three miles of sand by the side of the Ganges, like sand by the sea-shore. It was very good of the elephants not to sink into it – half the hackeries with our goods did, and could not come on for long. The Thanadar of the village arranged for fifteen boats to convey us. As usual we sent on a set of tents the night before. The first sight that struck us was these same tents on this side of the river and one solitary boat, so here we are, no tents pitched anywhere – eight in the morning, the sun getting high, and such a scene of confusion. All my furniture has been arriving on men's heads and then it stands. My dear sofa and armchair mixed up with the bullocks, hackeries, palanquins. My deer and Mrs C's lap-dog are behaving with great philosophy, so am I. I've got a footstool to sit upon, two umbrellas held over my head, and have sketched a small part of the scene [see p. 34]. Now I'm writing this with a pencil. Mrs C. says she won't try to be comfortable because it was so wicked of the Thanadar to put us in such a situation. Besides, we breakfasted on one cup of coffee at six, and have no chance of any more before twelve or one. Some of the elephants who had nearly swam to the other side have suddenly turned round. There is nothing but a bit of their heads to be seen. In case you don't know a howdah when you see it, there is mine. It is raised high on the elephant, backed by cushions. At this moment it is very usefully situated there; relief in the shape of two baskets of fruit which an angel of an indigo planter was sending on to the next encampment for me – and a servant has produced some biscuits and the gentlemen have looked up some boats.

Now I am finishing on the other side. My tent was pitching when I arrived so I took up my station in the tonjon under a tree while the

Stoppage by the side of the Ganges 43

operation was completed. The others, having no chance of theirs, went off breakfastless to hunt in the jungles. An hour later, I was frightened by hearing William call to me to know if the medicine chest had arrived. It instantly set me off thinking what medicine was good for a man that had been swallowed by a tiger. However nothing very serious was the matter. They had disturbed a nest of wild bees, upon which a cloud of them rose up and attacked them, and one gentleman had been very much stung about the head and declares he was never in such agony in his life. He thought they were going to sting him to death, and they drove him nearly mad. He was sure if they had gone on two minutes more he would have been in a madhouse for life. Thousands seem to have been round them all. William escaped with one or two stings, thanks to Ariffe having thrown his red shawl over him. At the same time the elephants giving signs of a tiger being near, but the bees fairly routed men and elephants and sent them away.

March 13th

There dear, I have killed my first tiger. They rallied against the bees, and we went to the same jungle to look for the one that they were sure they left there yesterday. It is in a rose bush jungle, which is always pretty. The elephants had hardly formed into a line and began to walk through it before there was a cry of tiger – and he bounded before all our elephants and got behind them. So then we had to turn back and walk through the jungle again, and before we were half way through it he sprang past us into the jungle towards another small patch of roses. He looked very grand then. We all hurried after him, the elephants stamping and screaming, and then he was shot at the first spring, within two yards of the one Mrs C. and I were upon. There is no safety but in the midst of the shooters and no feeling of danger with them.

I turned away my head when they shot because I have a natural dis-taste to see a large beast die – a sentiment I should not profess in this

35

country about a tiger. Ariffe slipped down the tail of William's elephant with a pistol to shoot it through the brain in case there should be any life left. Just then it made its dying struggle and the men sent such shrieks to him to get out of the way – they thought it was rallying for a spring. They went off to another jungle and I set off home with the dead tiger on a live elephant to guard me. Jones and Dulhoo, who had been following on my elephant, were both equally pleased with their own cleverness in having seen a tiger killed. The villagers made such a rejoicing over it as we passed and some of them asked if the Lady Sahib had killed it. We met a herd of wild buffaloes and a wild hog – but they did not take any notice of us.

March 14th

We are still in the same place. It is a very nice encampment in deep shade – and though the jungles are so extensive they will probably not find many tigers; the villagers have stories without end about them. They brought a very old man of 80 to the camp that he might report the story of what had happened to him the day before; he did it with much action and gesticulation. He and his grandsons were keeping their bullocks out at the edge of the jungle and thought they saw something move in it, upon which they went creeping up to it, then the tiger sprang past and seized the bullock, and then they shouted and he dropped it, but so much torn that it died. The gentlemen as usual went to rejoice over 'the Murray'. Another villager told us about the tiger they killed yesterday; at what time it used to drink, when it slept, and so on. They seem to have settled to lose so many bullocks in the course of the year – and that a tiger will very seldom take a man if he can get a bullock – I did not go out with them today. They killed a buffalo and I drew his head which was cut off and put under a tree. William says five minutes after it was killed nothing but its bones were left, all the natives eat its flesh, and cut it up with knives or sharp sticks or anything they could get at. They have such enormous horns and though they lie far back and look of no use, when they are exasperated and charge, they sometimes knock over a small elephant.

March 15th

They killed another buffalo today and found another tiger which got off into thick jungle. Captain C. has got a pair of buffalo horns, seven feet between them at the widest point. I sketched the body of one they brought home. I forgot to mention that my deer sate in my howdah

when they were shooting the tiger and did not care for the guns, he only opened his dark eyes rather wider.

We moved today four miles to a hideous open plain with nothing but white ants' nests to break it, and a burning sun beating on the tents and so, the thermometer being near ninety, I am a leetle hot. There is no road and I am waiting till the hackeries drop in with provisions before I have breakfast. There are jungles they dare not pass and jeels they cannot pass – and this my hungry hour. Another indigo planter has just sent me a live black sheep and a large pat of butter – if the sheep were a loaf I should be grateful. The others are shooting still. We have long been away from any post and it is a whole fortnight since I have had any tidings of George and Emily. He was growing very despotic when we left home – he may have committed any atrocity during our absence. He has probably cut off the heads of all the aide-de-camps.

We were half way through dinner yesterday when a servant came in to say there was a wild buffalo near the camp. Upon which, it being broad moonlight, and William the only one who had his gun loaded, he set off after it on foot like a madman, followed by the others like so many more madmen and by Mrs Cockerell and me like two mad women, because it was more than probable that they would only exasperate it and then it would be sure to charge and knock over anybody on foot. Ariffe, who was waiting behind me, simply observed, 'Captain Osborne do very foolish thing, Ladysheep. And you will do very foolish thing to follow him.' However, at the first shot William wounded him so much that he fell, and then he rallied again, and Mrs C. and I retreated towards the tent, not but what he was likely to charge that as anywhere else, particularly as almost all the servants who had been waiting on us and half the camp were in full chase after him. And altogether it was a very grand moonlight scene. However he took to the water and then William came up and shot him.

We have come four miles today and just after I had parted company with the shooters to go to the tents I fell in with that mosque, a real beauty to look at, but it was getting so hot I could only make a hurried sketch of it from the back of the elephant [see p. 37]. When I arrived I found the servants in commotion. The tents had been pitched in the night, and mine and the Cockerells' were under a great tree, where there was a wild bees' nest, and so many of the servants had been stung, and they were in such a fright they would all fly out, there was nothing for it but to break up the encampment. However, I was more afraid of the sun than the bees, and braved them for two hours with great impunity till our other tents came up. The impatience of wild bees is a new light to me, but if they get exasperated they fly out in thousands and sometimes follow the same person or elephant for miles.

March 16th. Gorrburreeba.

That is a true simple village name, so I give it to you, and as I lie on my sofa on one side of the tent, that is the view presented to me on the other. Though the mornings and evenings are still fresh and very unlike the same articles in Calcutta it is growing very hot in the middle of the day, and I believe all the camp sleeps except me. William has been in that attitude for the last two hours, it's very odd he has not got the cramp, and one bearer comes after another to fan him and he does not wake. Though the thermometer at this hour is ninety, a punkah bores me so when it is not pulled by invisible hands. I am still carrying on life without it. There is always some air blowing through the tent and the extreme heat only lasts from 2 to 5.

My deer is ruminating upon a shocking escape he has just had. He was playing outside the tent when a great pariah dog ran after him. Upon which he rushed into the tent and the dog rushed after him and eight bearers after the dog, altogether presenting a scene of the most intense interest. There are more tigers about here than anywhere we have yet been, but the infatuated creatures who go after them will not kill any. They inhabit jungles which are quite impenetrable to the elephants with howdahs. They must learn to be content with deer and buffaloes. The villagers here come out in crowds to look at us, never having seen European women. I take out my sketch book and look full at them and pretend to sketch them and they cover up their faces and run away as if a shot were fired among them – a very simple method of dispersing them. This is such a pretty encampment – the fern higher than our tents, growing among such beautiful trees. I could quite fancy myself in a large English park.

March 17th

We are going to move after dinner, for the moon is as bright as day now, and the sun begins to get hot before eight in the morning. However, they have been out shooting till near eleven, and went to a bit of jungle which was burnt last week when fifteen tigers came out of it, but they could not make their way far with the jungles near. Dulhoo looks perturbed at this new order of march and evidently thinks that somehow or other it will interfere with his dinner. It always amuses me to see all the separate castes with their separate fires cooking their messes. At night when we are among trees it is like the incantation scene in the *Freischütz* on a great scale. The servants who are not in waiting do not trouble themselves by wearing any particular quantity of clothes.

March 18th

We had only eight miles to move yesterday evening and as long as we stuck to the elephant nothing could be more satisfactory, but after we had gone two miles William and I, owing to the credulity of our dispositions, trusted to the natives' declaration that there was a good road for the tilbury and a guide who would run before and shew us the way. After we had driven a considerable distance with great difficulty, we found ourselves in the middle of a jungle where there was no road at all, and the guide quite innocent of knowing anything about the tents or how to get us out again. I thought of the fifteen wandering tigers as I saw the jungles burning in every direction round us. I thought still more of an enormous wild buffalo that was swimming towards us across a small jeel. We were passing at a foot's pace – it was impossible to get on faster. I was never so shaken and jolted, to say nothing of running against various trees because there was not room to pass them. If we had had a mere mortal horse and tilbury they never could have held together. We did get home at last or I should not now be writing to you, but of all the wild things we have yet done that was the wildest. We were three hours and a half about the eight miles, and I was never more glad than when we caught sight of some of our elephants. We had to cross a river, when the horse stood in a small boat in the most exemplary manner, and we were quite uncertain all the time whether we were not going away from our tents instead of towards them.

March 19th
We are resting here today. William suggested to the man whom I have sketched with that quantity of hair that it would be as well if he were to have it cut, to which he assented, but said that his caste was so low nobody in the camp would touch him, which is quite true. They would not take anything out of his hand. The other day I heard sounds of altercation when Dulhoo, Jones, Myra and Sorga (the house maid) were setting off on an elephant. Dulhoo said he could not sit by Sorga because he should lose caste by it, upon which I suggested he should sit as a servant behind me, to which he made no objection.

March 20th & 21st. Barcool.
At last we have got an immense packet of letters, ten from George and Emily and a great many English ones written in October, five months ago.* It seemed very odd to be reading them in the heart of the jungles – but I was very glad to have them. To be sure nothing can be less satisfactory than the communication between us all. 'Why do not you tell me what you are doing *now?*' is the feel I am always left with. I had none from you this time, but that is no reason against your having written twenty letters which will all arrive in time, but the twentieth probably the first. And somebody mentioned you are at Motcombe, very busy about schools. We have just been building a beautiful school in Barrackpore park and George writes me he has got the model of a schoolmaster who speaks English and wears spectacles. I dare say you go to the useless expense of giving *your* children clothes at Xmas. *Our* children do not wear any. This is one of the little beneficial hints I am

* These letters must have come via the sea route, round the Cape of Good Hope. An alternative 'overland' mail route via Suez was just being established by Lieutenant Thomas Waghorn, RN. This took only two months.

41

able to give you from my superior travelled views. Next Xmas you will know what to do.

As they went out deer shooting this afternoon I thought I would go to sketch in the village, and for the first time set off on foot to walk a quarter of a mile. You would have laughed at the result of my experiment. Dulhoo had taken such pains to impress the villagers with my greatness, I found as fast as I passed any they threw themselves flat with their faces in the dust, and there was I in solitary majesty, one servant carrying my book, another my pencils, a third an armchair, a fourth a footstool, a fifth an umbrella, and all those prostrate bodies round me – so I went home in utter desperation and contented myself with drawing our cooking tent which we have never got up the hill.

March 22nd. Malda.

We are by way of being encamped at Malda, but we happen to be three miles from it and nothing within sight but an uninhabited factory. They had their last day's shooting today. We leave the jungles tomorrow. The Magistrate here since we have been within twenty-five miles of him has been sending us vegetables and fruit, and in the gratitude of our hearts we asked him to dinner. I am still very grateful and they say he is an excellent Magistrate and understands the natives' ways. I dare say he does – I am sure he does not understand ours. If you think you have ever seen a vulgar man, come 15,000 miles and see him and then you will know your mistake. At Government House that sort of man never speaks at all, and with the best intentions I was quite puzzled to understand half of what he said. 'I hear he has become a member of the juwaub club,' he remarked of somebody. 'Of what club?' I innocently asked, and then it appeared that juwaub being the Hindoostani word for answer, a gentleman who has been proposed and been refused is said to be juwaubed. I shall naturally say when I return to England Mr — has become a member of the juwaub club.

However, this same man conferred two signal benefits upon me. He told me that in the factory there was a very fine black marble chimney piece, stolen from Gom in the first instance, and afterwards bought by a European, who now offers to sell house and chimney piece for £100. The house is half in ruins, but the chimney piece quite perfect in every sense of the word, and so I told him to try and get it for George, and we will pack it up bodily and send it to England. I see it in the hall at Knightsbridge – with my long tiger skin as a rug – beautiful! The other cleverness the creature showed me was in having a large tattie* made to

* A screen of fragrant grass.

42

cover one side of our tent, and it is kept wetted all day, and does make the air cool or cooler, but before we get home I expect that an oven will be an object of admiration to us, not unmixed with envy.

March 23rd

We are at what was Gaur today, the remains being exceedingly small and diminishing every year, for it is in the domain of natives who have no respect for antiquity. We passed through an old gateway that was quite beautiful, but I did not stop to sketch it because William observed with an air of infinite satisfaction, 'I told them to pitch our tents in Gaur, and you will have such a quantity of things to sketch, you must not stop now'. So we went on a mile and found our tents pitched in what might have been called a very ugly English orchard – not a building within sight. The tent pitcher not being a good Musselman, and having no taste for the picturesque, has set us down between two grand objects, the Gateway and the Golden Mosque. Dulhoo is of course gone to his dinner and will not mind. Ariffe has already made a tour of Mosques and he says the two fine ones are within a mile of us – so when the sun will let us, at half-past-four, we shall go after them, come back to dinner, and then go and have a good look at the gateway by moonlight.

We parted from the Cockerells last night. They mean to travel back to Calcutta, and will only be three nights and two days about what will take us ten or twelve, but very few women at this time of year could stand such fatigue. The heat is growing awful in the middle of the day. That dear vulgar man's tattie is of use to us, but by the time we reach Calcutta it will be an even bet whether we are human creatures or cinders.

There, dear, you have seen how busy I have been this afternoon, and I am perfectly frantic with those pitchers because if they had put our tents where they ought we should not only have been in the midst of a colony of monkeys, but I might have sketched in that old Mosque during all the heat of the day. As it is I could only do a little bit of the middle aisle; the sides are covered with carved black marble. It is quite clear to me that our chimney piece was stolen from there – in fact there are nothing and nobody to prevent any individual who has strength from taking up the whole Mosque and conveying it away. I think that the man who is governing India should pass a law against that. One side of it is beautifully ornamented – you see the sort of thing.

There are other magnificent remains of Mosques about, but they are going fast to decay. There are heaps of monkeys about here and in their

43

manners they assume a tone of careless superiority towards us which is rather humiliating. I wonder whether they really are the cleverest animal of the two – perhaps they built that Mosque. I am sure I do not know who else in the country could.

We found an enormous skeleton of a snake – Ariffe said a boa constrictor, and that it was thirty feet long. I trust that none of its relations are alive, because we shall hardly have room for them in our tents. In these remote parts where there are only monkeys to comment upon it, William and I have taken to going about upon an elephant in a very dégagée manner, nothing but a large stuffed crimson cushion upon its back, without the howdah; and upon this we sit, very much as if we had been in an Irish jaunting car. The animal goes twice as fast and as smoothly – it is the common natural way of being carried on them – and in these short expeditions much less trouble. But we think Dulhoo looks severe about it, as if he thought it undignified, so upon the march we go in state.

The thermometer is ninety-six in this tent at the moment – it feels so hot sometimes I think I cannot bear it five minutes longer. However this does not last long, at four it grows cooler. All our camp keep well, the few cases of illness we have had I treated with great medical skill. The natives always send the most moving petitions for medicine the instant they are ill, but seldom swallow it unless they like the taste. Being told of that fact, I made Jones see them swallow it, and suspect I have heard much less of illness in consequence.

The Guddry Mosque must have been a magnificent one in its day – a very little way from the other – and there are some fine tombs about it. After that we went home, had some dinner and when the moon got up set off again upon an elephant after the gateway that we so rashly passed in the morning. On our way we met the Cockerells in their palanquin out of which they were not to stir for the next sixteen hours, then rest during the great heat of the day, and then go on for sixteen more. So we expended a great deal of pity upon them and they probably expended as much upon us, with our prospect of eight or ten days grilling before we get to shut-up rooms and punkahs.

I was baffled about sketching the gateway. I could not get enough out of the shade of the trees to see the lines on the paper, but so beautiful a ruin as the thing itself I never yet saw. The arch is such an enormous height and immense trees seem to grow out of the walls, with their roots hanging over; and large towers inlaid in those same walls with remains of that frittery carving which I think so beautiful.

Those people must have been so very magnificent in what they did before we Europeans came here with our bad money-making ways. We have made it impossible for them to do more, and have let all they accomplished go to ruin. All our excuse is, that we do not oppress the natives so much as they oppress each other – a fact about which I have my suspicions. And at all events Runjeet Singh is the sort of man who if he has fallen into the misfortune some morning of cutting off a thousand architects' heads – would have made them build something magnificent first. It was very clever of us to come this way, because it is not the usual road and though everybody talks of the ruins of Gaur, very few go to see them. Indeed we have come a great part of the way without finding even the pretence of a road.

March 24th. Sureeb.

This is the last place we encamp at upon the side of the Ganges, and a remarkably uninteresting looking place it is. William and I went out for our afternoon's exercise . . . Dulhoo had hung over the crimson cushion the long scarlet trappings which are embroidered with gold, and looked grimly complacent at the halo of splendour he had thrown round us. The Chief of the Brahmins in this part of the world sent word he was coming to make his salaam, a fact which Dulhoo evidently considered of immense importance, and correspondingly in the evening he did come in a tonjon with an umbrella held over his head, and a set of ragged servants after him. He, William and I, sat gravely down on three chairs in front of the tents, and there he offered me a bag of rupees – which I was to touch, not take, but the touch was to show I would take them if I wanted them. As it happened I did, very much, for we cannot get any notes changed. However the high integrity of my nature prevailed and with an air of benign condescension I only put my hand upon them. He left some sweetmeats for the servants, the division of which kept the whole camp in a wrangle for three whole hours. We heard Dulhoo more than usually disputatious and tiresome about his share of a cake made of sugar.

March 25th. Comra.

This is rather dull for you, dear. We crossed the Ganges this morning and have got back to Comra again, and I wrote to you about Comra before. We had a long march and as we did not like to wait while the elephants swam across, got into the tilbury on the other side and came across a succession of plowed fields where there was not even the pretence of a road. An indigo planter, or as the natives call him in their language, 'a blue fellow', came to speak to William the other day. Some of these planters live all the year round without seeing another European, they seem to have forgotten how to speak English. Now and then in a good season and with good speculation they make immense sums of money.

The nearer we get to Calcutta the more this shocking old furnace heats up. From 1 to 4 the outer air is really quite scorching, and as in tents it is impossible to shut air out, I am reduced to wish myself between walls again. The thermometer is ninety-five at this moment. I keep writing on because if I were to think how hot I am I should die of it. William very cleverly goes to sleep while the sun is doing its worst, and we have eight months of this hot season to come. My spirit quails when I think of it.

March 26th. Dewan Serai.
There is a purely domestic scene. The camp is always followed by a quantity of pariah dogs, half-wild creatures who belong to nobody. One has followed us about all the way from Barrackpore, rather a handsome one but perhaps slightly related to the Jackal tribe. As he attached himself particularly to William, it has required the united energies of the 260 people who comprise the camp to keep him and my deer

separate. The instant the dog looked that way everybody began shrieking at him. This evening both animals were missing, and this was the attitude in which I found them. The deer always walks straight up to any animal it sees, the impertinence of the proceeding was too much for the spirit of the pariah dog, and they have been licking each other's faces. I asked why this place is called Serai, thinking that there was perhaps a house near at hand full of what would be reckoned here respectable females. But they showed me a large tank of water and sand: that was the reason it was called Serai and now I wonder why. Whoever digs a tank, or causes a tank to be dug, is supposed when he dies to go straight to heaven.

March 27th. Morshadabad.
Again we have a house over our heads and this time I do not despise it. To have the outward air shut out and punkahs pulled over our heads after the baking of the last few days makes us feel positively chilly. We arrived to breakfast at Mr Cunningham's; and Mr Melville will send a carriage to take us to his house to dine and sleep. There is something very dull and civilised in that. In the meantime, having some of my camp activity still left, I have been to see the oddest building I ever saw, the size of a small village and it must be substantial because it is old, but it all looks as if it were made out of talc and tinsel. The tombs of some of the Nawaub's ancestors are there.

I sketched one in an arch of an enormous gallery that goes round an octagon building where there is another tomb which looks upon a larger scale, like the sort of thing one used to fabricate out of paper and tinsel to look pretty in a baby house. The one I sketched was either of talc or glass. The other sketch I made was one of many great shields which have a tank of water in front [see p. 48]. A great deal of that is talc. The rounds are the part of a rhinocerous they call a shield. All the solid part of the building is black – there is a large court and another great gallery which surrounds it all.

The great Musselman feast of the Moharrum is next week and they were preparing this building for it. As if the shield were not tawdry enough they were inserting scarlet and yellow cotton to set off the pattern on it. Mr Cunningham says when it is lighted up with thousands of little lamps it is really splendid. The pillars of the building are black but ornamented with some kind of shiny stuff. They made no objection of my sitting in the outer court to sketch. One told Mr C. they would rather I should walk than be carried in a tonjon, and I was going to leave it outside, but the native priest in authority would not let me.

47

The Imambara

The Nawaub is in a state of the highest felicity because in exchange for the magnificent presents he sent the King* of shawls, ivory and silver things, the King has sent him the Order of the Guelf. Of all the puzzling workings of the human mind, I think one of the most puzzling is that which makes the Nawaub of Morshadabad fancy he likes the Order of the Guelf. But he sends for Mr Melville once or twice a week to know how he shall wear it, and how he should comport himself when he gets it – and condescendingly observes he likes the look of his new palace so much now it is finished, he shall tell his own people to run him up another like it. If he meant to pique the builders he could not have said a cleverer thing.

My dear, I am at Mr Melville's now. We left it to him to settle whether we had better go on by land or water – and he has settled water. The river is so shallow here we can go in country boats called budgerows – and the prospect is a hot one, but less appalling than travelling dak day and night – or a twelve days' march. Six days it usually takes by water, but we have taken an extra set of men that we may do it in three or four. Having settled this I have just got a letter from George saying the heat of the river will be unbearable and we had better travel by night on land. However, we still mean to try the river, and I hope he will not cut off our heads when we arrive. As we can only take a few of the servants we have told Dulhoo that he must march home to take care of the others and the plate, all we leave him being two tea-spoons. The Nawaub sent us his boats, so large, we should have stuck upon a sand bank till the rains.

March 28th. On board the Budgerow.
There is something shippy and bad in the look of that, is not there? and that is all the prospect I have at this present writing [see p. 50]. Myra is sitting in the attitude in which she usually passes the day when she is not actively employed in holding out a pin for Jones to stick into me, and I believe very few ayahs do much more – except that they actually stick the pins in – not only through the clothes but the victim who wears them. There are only two rooms in each of our budgerows – Jones sleeps on the sofa in the sitting room. They are not very small, and now the green blinds are all open, the wind blows through and it promises to be less hot than I expected. To be sure we have not come on board till the hottest hours of the day are past. William's boat is rather smaller and lighter than mine, and if he chooses to go on at once to Calcutta without waiting for me I cannot stop him. However the cooking boat sticks close to me and he

* William IV

49

will hardly leave that. We have a goat upon which he and the deer and I are all dependent for milk. I hope we shall have no storm, for this river is like a small sea, and would make nothing of swallowing up our small boat. We saw a man today by the river side, left by his affectionate friends to die there.

This time of year the wind will be against us all the way, so sometimes they row and sometimes they tow us. The boatmen are a fine, hardworking race of people. Their singing is more like singing and less like screaming, than anything I have heard in India.

March 29th. Morshadabad.
We landed last night, for the boatmen anchor when it grows dark. We would not let them be near a village for that ensures a noisy night, but we had our dinner table put out upon a very handsome sand-bank. It looked so odd when we were walking at a little distance to see a table with silver plate and candlesticks and nothing to relieve it of any kind,

for the budgerows were hid by the bank. The insects did not plague us the least and we played at écarté with great success, with nobody but Pariah dogs to look on.

There is a moon which rose at two yesterday morning, and the boatmen have worked seventeen hours – very much to the satisfaction of ourselves and the Musselman servants, but to the utter desperation of the Hindoos, whose caste will not let them cook on board a boat. So some went more than twenty-four hours without eating. It is lucky that the boats we pass are so strange and picturesque and no two alike, for there has been nothing else to look at – the shores are all sand without human habitation. William had outsailed us while we were all asleep – and we got aground, a shocking situation. However, at twelve in the day we got near enough for the cooking boat to transport him and the chess board into my premises. We are getting on so fast we ought tomorrow to be in water deep enough for a steamer – if there is one to send to meet us – but the few there are are almost all employed in towing out large ships.

March 30th and 31st

I did not write yesterday because the water does not afford many incidents. Again we passed a child left to die by the riverside. This afternoon we found the steamer waiting for us and our three boats are lashed on to it, and we shall be at Barrackpore I hope by eleven tomorrow morning. We are anchored now for the night. There are some good buildings we passed today, but what I have not the least idea. The steamer went too fast to make much of sketching them. A missionary came off from Culna to ask for a passage on board the steamer to Calcutta. William and I were taken by his look and asked him to dinner, and it answered to us. He had been living for seventeen years in the Rajah of ——'s city – the only European there – who allows him to have as many schools and make as many converts as he can – and he seemed satisfied with what he had done in both ways. Yesterday he had actually seen a woman carried off by an aligator and not an effort was made to save her. He seemed clever and sensible and to be sure if ever there was a country where missionaries are wanted this is it.

There was an official account last week of one district, under our dominion too, where every year at the time the crops are sown a certain number of creatures are sacrificed and their limbs spread about the land. Sometimes they are literally cut up alive. Three weeks ago the European resident there rescued twenty-eight – some of them had been bought as children and brought up for the purpose – eight girls he has sent down to the orphan school here. They would have been sacrificed this spring. Some of the future victims are allowed to marry but their families as well as themselves are sacrificed in time. All this is a new discovery and Government will take what measures they can that are safe to stop such horrors, but such customs can only be done away with by degrees.

April 1st. Barrackpore.
And now, dear, I shall finish this off and send it as soon as I can. You will never read half that I have written and I think it will cure you of wishing for letters from me for some time.

We landed this morning at eleven, and found George and Emily here to meet us, and both looking particularly well and prosperous. In this country to have been absent for near two months without one trouble or fright of any kind is a blessing to be thankful for. Certainly this expedition has quite answered to me in point of pleasure. Then, I am rather proud of having seen a tiger killed because except Mrs Cockerell there is not another woman in India who has, I believe.

This park looks very nice indeed, just now, the grass and trees are such a beautiful green at this time of the year and we shall be alone for the next three days. I am persuaded that if the beasts we have left were a little tamer and the people we are going to were a little wilder, the improvement would be remarkable.

As I have been consistently pompous about my sketches from beginning to end, I may as well say now that I will give you great credit if you make some of them out – but then, dear, I had no time to do anything really. Besides writing all this to you I wrote to Emily and George every day whether there was post or no post – and besides that a journal to my family in England, of which this is very much a repetition. I guess then there were gaps in the middle of the day – and you who sit in a chair and write on a table will never grasp the difficulty of drawing from an elephant's back unless you will pass one morning on that of the sophisticated animal in the Regents Park. Nevertheless, put this in some cupboard for me when I come home, for don't you know, one likes to see what one *has* done. I was going to add 'Mind the cockroaches don't eat it' (we always say that when we put anything away). The deer with its usual taste has instantly adopted the habits of civilised life and is established on the sofa in the drawing room. The Pariah dog is marching down with Dulhoo and the two greyhounds. And now, dearest, goodbye and God bless you,

Yours most affectionately
Frances H. Eden

Second Journal

The Progress through the Upper Provinces

Fanny did not resume her illustrated journal to Eleanor Grosvenor until October 1837. The journey on which she then embarked with Emily, George, William and 12,000 others had two particular ends in view. George wanted to visit the Upper Provinces of India to see that they were being administered well. It was also important that he build on the treaty of friendship signed by his predecessor Lord William Bentinck with Ranjit Singh in 1831, to protect India's northwest borders.

George's uncle, Lord Minto, had as Governor-General first opened relations with Afghanistan in 1809, signing an alliance with the ruler Shah Shuja against the French. After Napoleon's downfall, the French were no more to be feared. There remained Russia which had already swallowed up all the Persian possessions on the south of the Caucasus, as well as part of the Ottoman empire. British trade missions had found Russian agents in favour at the Persian court, and Russian influence seeping into Afghanistan. All Asia was aware of this growing Russian penetration into the states bordering India.

Lord William Bentinck had left a Minute for his successor. 'From the days of Peter the Great to the present time,' he wrote, 'the views of Russia have been turned to the obtaining possession of that part of central Asia which is watered by the Oxus, and joins the eastern shore of the Caspian. The latest accounts from Kabul state that they are building a fort between the Caspian and Khiva. This is the best line of their operation against India, but it can only be considered at present as a very distant speculation . . .'

Lord Auckland and his advisers hoped that the threat of aggression would continue to be a distant speculation, but nobody could be sure. Before he had left London, he had had long discussions with Sir John Cam Hobhouse, the President of the Board of Control, and had received perfectly explicit instructions. He was to do everything in his power to build a rampart of friendly states round the north-west provinces of India. This meant alliances with the rulers of those territories.

The most important was Ranjit Singh, the ruler of the Sikh kingdom of the Punjab, the old Lion of the North. Ranjit had had his own period of acquisitiveness; he had taken Peshawar from the Afghans in 1833 and had only recently been sharply pulled up by the British for 'casting covetous eyes on territories in the possession of his neighbours, the Amirs of Sind.' He had been bidden to keep his hands off his neighbours' possessions and stay on his own side of the Sutlej river. The hard-headed old Sikh had accepted the instruction; the British were more useful to him as allies than enemies. So the Punjab could be more or less depended upon. The great problem was Afghanistan. The weak and ineffectual Shah Shuja had been ousted by Dost Mohammed Khan in 1826 and fled to live among the Sikhs. Dost Mohammed was a warrior who also had a shrewd political sense. He sent a letter to the new Governor-General of India, congratulating him on his safe arrival. He hoped Lord Auckland would advise him how best to govern Afghanistan and how to get Peshawar back from the Sikhs. The Governor-General answered in equally friendly terms and ended with the firm statement that it was not the practice of the British Government to take sides in disputes between independent states. George sent Alexander Burnes, one of the pioneers of 'the Great Game', to report on the situation in Kabul, and in the meantime pressed ahead with the trip to Ranjit Singh. A few weeks after they all set out, the Persians laid siege to Herat in Western Afghanistan, encouraged by the Russians. This fed the Russophobia that possessed William Macnaghten and George's other close advisers. When Burnes reported the arrival of a Russian envoy at Kabul in December 1837, Macnaghten started to urge George that it might be necessary to depose Dost Mohammed and put Shah Shuja in his place. Burnes returned from Kabul in 1838 but was unable to prevent this misguided policy from taking firm root – the very sort of intervention that George had told Dost Mohammed he would not countenance.

This failure of judgement on George's part has overshadowed and obscured his undoubtedly humane, enlightened and conscientious rule in India itself. He was a firm advocate of wider education for Indians. He did all he could to alleviate a drought-induced famine which had overtaken the Upper Provinces while he was travelling through them. He realised that the best hope for avoiding repetitions of such horrors was to increase the irrigation works, and his plan for the Ganges Canal was eventually completed in 1854.

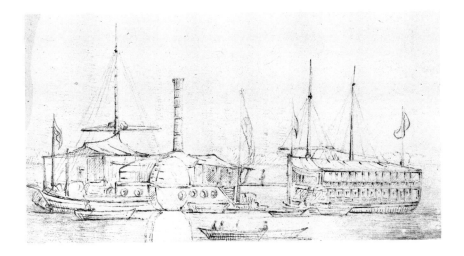

October 21st 1837 – on board the flat.

I wish I knew, dear, whether my last sketch book and Journal bored you very much, and whether you counted it as three or four letters which I meant you should do – and whether a strong qualm of bore will come over you at the sight of another and whether you will not wish that India had never been born, if it is to be rammed down your throat in such a detailed way. However, as we are fairly off now on our up country journey, I feel it due to myself and the occasion, to draw and write and as usual, poor dear, you shall be my victim.

I finished off Calcutta to you in a letter I sent a week ago. We left it this morning at half past six and a great many came to see us off. I think there was something awful and touching in the quantity of leave-taking we went through on the Ghat, and there was a great deal of martial shew, and guns doing their salutes, and we, stepping gracefully aboard, 'clad in paradoxical emotion', the suit in which the immortal author of Santo Sebastiano always clothed his heroes. Altogether, it was a striking Governor-General parting scene and would have brought tears into Theodore Hook's* eyes.

We are in a flat. I have so entirely lost my recollections of other countries, I cannot remember whether flats are peculiar to this, but for a thing that is to move about on the water they are very comfortable inventions. The noisy active business of life is carried on on board the steamer which tows us. We have a very comfortable set of rooms, nobody on board but ourselves, the aide-de-camps and Dr Drummond, Chance, the Lemur, and Gazelle. Tonight we shall be in the Soonderbuns – a place

* Contemporary novelist of the fashionable world

devoted to tigers and fevers, a sort of salt water creek bordered by jungles. We are driven this way by the unwonted shallowness of the river. It is so pleasant to be moving again, and I long to be at Benares and under tents once more. George has got a strange idea in his head that a house is a more solid and comfortable thing to live in – he will cure of that.

October 22nd, 23rd & 24th

We are almost out of the Soonderbuns now. Since we came into them, except for a few aligators, I do not think we have seen a living thing. The boatmen say they have seen two tigers but they owed it to themselves to say that. There seem to be no insects, no birds, no human thing. Sometimes the creek turns so shortly we seem to be in a lake surrounded by woods, and sometimes it is so narrow, the boughs of the trees sweep the deck. Yesterday at one fell swoop they carried away all George's blinds and half William's hookah.

There is another flat following us with a great many of the living implements of Indian government on board and their little descendants. Mr and Mrs Colvin – you know them already – the private secretary and secretaress, Mr and Mrs Macnaghten –he is the Government secretary and I am fond of him – only any little trifle it may please our black brethren to bestow upon us, he takes away with rather greater celerity than it can be given. Mr and Mrs Torrens – he is the son of Sir H. Torrens, is clever and a good amateur actor, and knows people in England we know, which is an advantage not often to be met with. She is handsome with a look of Lord Robert, which makes my heart warm to her, and is the most wonderful lady player on the harp I have ever heard. But of course the heat and damp crack all the strings and eventually the sounding board and it is a talent almost wasted in India. I only wonder that we do not all crack, now I think of it. There are moments when we all feel a little cracked. Captain and Mrs Hawkins – he is the man, who as far as I can make out, is every day to kill enough sheep and to boil enough vegetables to feed the 10,000 people who comprise the camp. She was very pretty and is still rather pretty, and is written about in the accounts of the fancy balls as 'the beautiful Mrs H. in an appropriate costume'.

Then there is an old General Casement who has been in India any imaginable number of years – a very gentlemanlike old man, with a wife in England who spends all his money, and he a shade angry with all the other inhabitants of the flat, because they have children, ayahs, Persian cats and parrots. But ayahs are his supreme aversion because they smoke

and chatter too, and he informed us that Mrs Macnaghten meant to take five to dress herself.

We shall be short of milk. Driven to frenzy in the middle of the night by the bleating of a kid, William inconsiderately called out to have it killed. The Hindu servants are half starved because their religion will not let them cook on the water and the fear of tigers keeps them from landing. Gazelle can get no green food and hates the flat, and wishes we had never thought of going up the country. We suffer much less from heat than I expected. I sit a great deal on deck and I am trying to sketch with colour chalks, as you see.

October 25th & 26th

That is the lemur and his nursery maid. He has just been washed and always spreads himself out like an eagle to be dried. The instant a servant has done his share of waiting he slips off his fine clothes and unless he is busy cooking, takes to that active manner of passing the day. As far as we can make out the inhabitants of the other flat have taken the same method of passing their time. When we came to anchor yesterday evening at seven o'clock, William went on board on a domiciliary visit, and found all the ladies were gone to bed and a very harmonious time prevailed among the others. General Casement spoke highly of the general behaviour of the bab-bies, and candidly about Mrs Macnaghten's Persian cat. Mrs Macnaghten, who was accused of having five ayahs on board, had sent one back, she being suspected of having drunk a bottle and a half of brandy. Parties were running rather high as to whether that was not a jealous calumny of the other ayahs.

We have not got on fast today, the river has been so shallow and the turning so sharp. The steamer has been generally scraping against the bottom and bumping against the bank, and not being its proper element was naturally puzzled to find itself on dry land. The country on each side is ugly and flat, as with the exception of Rajmahal it will be for the next thousand miles. We trust for the picturesque, to the cities and inhabitants.

We are stopping for the night at Camerolly and taking in coals, and the servants are all cooking on shore and the natives chattering and screaming round them – such a complication of noises. I forgot to tell you, dearest, that the very day after I sent my letter thanking you for those invaluable gowns, I got your letter about them, and a treasure of a letter it was. I like to know that you are all going on doing the same things and that it is only to us that England and English life have burnt themselves out in their sockets.

October 27th

. . . We get on much slower than we expected and George, cut off from his papers and his office boxes and his 'members in council', has a sort of deposed Governor-General feel which makes him impatient. Nevertheless, invitations to a ball have reached us from Brigadier Richards and the officers of the station at . . . I fancy this is the beginning of a constant course of dancing we are going through till we reach the Himalayas, and the horrid thing is we have but one dancing young lady with us, Mrs Colvin's niece. I think it would be fitting if George would learn to walk through the minuet de la cour. Emily or I could take it in turn to follow with the reigning brigadier of the station.

I like the life aboard this flat, except during the very sunny hours of the day. We sit out a great deal on deck, and I find I can write and draw and work. I have not worked for months before, from sheer langour. Now I fill odd moments with a great piece of tapestry. General Casement and Mr Macnaghten came on board this evening. As usual, all their ladies had gone to bed. We think there is something wrong about the apply jelly they have at breakfast. A mysterious allusion was made to it by Mr Macnaghten, which was hastily nipped in the bud by General Casement.

October 28th

. . . A Mr Graham and a Mr Lushington came to see us and we took them with us back to their own station further up the river. Mr Lushington was still in College at Calcutta when we first arrived. Before he came out to India he had been for some years at Naples, then at Paris, then in London. As soon as he was out of College, he was sent off to a station where there were but three Europeans besides himself, not a woman to speak to. That is what happens to half the young writers* – some are quite alone, no other European within reach – and in a climate where for some months they can hardly get out of the house, and why they do not go melancholy mad I cannot conceive. Some do come back to Calcutta in a frightfully nervous state of health, some take to the life but then they grow dreamy and stupid, not that that signifies so long as they are happy, and there is no country in which people may be left to dream with greater impunity. The Indigo planters are worse off still – some really forget how to speak English. We stopped again at Boglio in the middle of the day for George to go and see the jail, but it was too sunny for us to land. The sun goes on being a shocking powerful old fellow but the air is much cooler than when we left Calcutta.

October 29th
This is Sunday, which in this sort of life is very difficult to remember. The last we heard of Mr Wimberley, the chaplain who set off with his family in a country boat a month before us, was that during that month he had not got on ten miles a day, the stream was so strong against him. So when he arrives at Benares is very doubtful. There, dear, you see Chance and his attendant, a most devoted man, I could conscientiously recommend him to anybody who wants a head nurse. Chance infinitely prefers him to any of us, and in that attitude they pass the greatest part of the day, a great example to the Lemur and his boy, who are constantly falling out. Gazelle sticks to his rule of never allowing a native to touch him, and they hurt his feelings and mine by calling him Guzzle, knowing no better, poor ignorant creatures. The other man is William's hookahburdar and how he answers it to his conscience to let his hookah stand there without its snake I cannot imagine [see p. 63].

Mr Colvin, Mr Macnaghten and General Casement came on board this evening and had fished up some business from the depths of the river evidently very refreshing to George's feelings. His is certainly a most trying situation. How can he know while we are bumping on a sandbank that we might not have had an opportunity of seizing for his own good the territories of Ram Rum Bohum? We are dignified with the other steamer because it tried to pass us and nearly ran us down

* Junior civil servants in the East India Company.

today. We are getting within sight of the Rajmahal Hills and William and I are beginning to grow tiresome with our reminiscences.

October 30th

. . . We are at Rajmahal this evening, landed and took a walk. Those dear old ruins look beautiful, so do the hills. George and Emily are quite properly struck by them. We went to the place where we were in camp and it does not seem as if a blade of grass has been moved since, and there in the middle of the ruins we found people waiting for us, with heaps of English letters. Such a pleasure – the latest we have had, the 17th of July. There might have been one from you, dearest, but there was not. Your peculiar post did not come in. No fault of yours, you are a real writing treasure, and they say you have been at East Combe,* which is nice for you – you told me in your last letter that you were thinking of going.

All everybody says about our young Queen is excessively interesting. It must have been such a strange feel to her at first, as if she were acting a play on a great scale, and she seems to be having great success in her part. I can fancy the Duchess of Kent must be very proud of the success of her work. And now I can write no more about India today. I never can after reading many English letters; a large English cloud rolls over everything here.

November 1st

Myra woke me this morning out of a remarkably satisfactory sleep to look at that – you know the sort of early sky nobody has any business to see, and three great rocks in the middle of the river which had evidently no business to be there – the Colgong rocks, which some odd freak of the Ganges transported into the middle of it.

I did not write yesterday partly from idleness and partly because the banks were so pretty. I passed the most part of the day looking at them. Now we are out of sight of the hills and have done with anything like beauty of country, and trust to beauty of town. You remember Ariffe, of course. You will be sorry to hear he has one fault, he wants resource about finding food for Gazelle. How he is to make it grow aboard this flat I do not exactly know but he ought.

I heard a shriek of laughter on deck last night just as we were going to bed, and called up to William to know what was the matter. Myra was arguing with the Lemur boy, whose head had been turned in the

* The home in Kent of Fanny's eldest sister Eleanor, the Countess of Buckinghamshire.

morning by Captain Champneys having given him a red and gold dress like the other servants, which in his caste he has no possible right to. His first démarche, with the Lemur clinging round his neck, was to make his salaam to George. At night, having picked up Gazelle and the Lemur he insisted on putting on his fine dress and going on shore to show himself off, much to Myra's vehement indignation, whenever her screams of laughing would give her breath to express it. There is a story extant which I believe is entirely a composition of William's, only everybody chooses to believe it, that Captain MacGregor and Captain Cunningham were kept yesterday waiting on shore, and when they asked why the boat did not come sooner, they were told it could not because the 'Lemur Sahib' wanted it to put him and his servant on shore for a run. So Cunningham Sahib must wait.

. . . We passed a little island today literally covered with pelicans – hundreds of them – not one inch of ground between them.

November 2nd. Monghyr.
We got here early this morning and have been passing a very busy day. A turn of the river has brought us a sight of the blue hills again. This is a curious old town with a fort and some good old buildings about. We could not land till the afternoon because of that burning old sun, who was in one of its most immoderate fits of shining, but we were surrounded by boats full of birds and birdcages, work boxes, straw bonnets and baskets, and buffalo horn necklaces. The Monghyr people are evidently geniuses. There was a work-table whose shadow is still over my mind, but I could not buy it, with a march in prospect, for any bulky article takes a separate man to carry it, and Byrne would naturally have dwaumed away at the sight of this. The three Europeans (or Eur*a*peans, as Emily's maid insists on calling them), came on board to talk Indian sense to George, the only European residents there. One of them is a son of Ld. Strathallan, who is going to be married to the only young lady there as soon as the Bishop comes back to marry them. He is up country and must return this way.

At half past three we landed and found all the manufactures of the place put together in a tent. The playthings were very ingenious. We stayed there while George went over the gaol, when the prisoners seem to have looked more wicked and more miserable than even prisoners need to look. Then all the equipages of the place were mustered, in the shape of three buggies and a carriage drawn by bullocks. George and Mr Brown, the great man there, got into one buggy, Emily and Captain MacGregor into another, William and I in the third, and we set off after a boiling spring five miles from the station. The drive was perfectly beautiful, so very wild, grey rocky hills all round us, not the least like any Indian scenery I have seen before, and the spring boiled and bubbled and scalded one's hand as a boiling spring should. A Brahmin lived near it and he liberally let me have some leaves for Gazelle off his peepul tree, though it is considered a sacred tree.

We saw Mr and Mrs Torrens straying about – Mrs Torrens told us that the other ladies were dreadfully peeved because General Casement had bought all kinds of pretty things for Mrs Hawkins and had offered them nothing. Mrs Macnaghten's parrot turns out much cleverer than all the children . . .

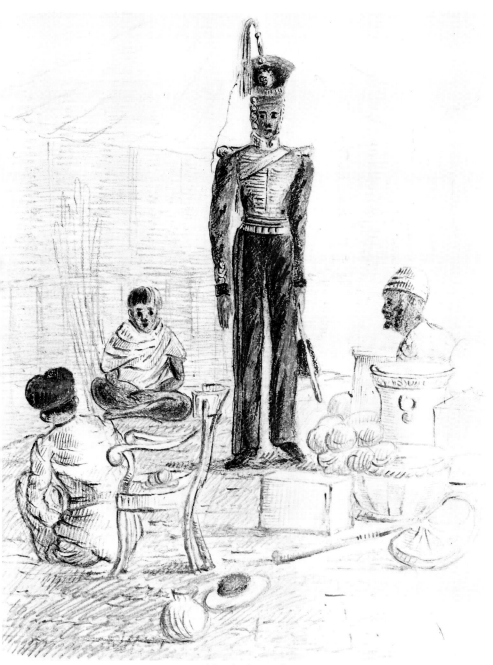

'Our bodyguard'

November 4th

The sides of the river were beautiful today from the crowds of natives all in their holyday dresses, with baskets of fruit and vegetables which the Ganges was to *look at* till sunset and then to wash. It is one of their festivals which will last three days. It is grown strange to me to see people clothed at all. They are all here wrapped round in chuddahs of every possible variety of colours, even the little children with only part of their faces peeping out, with bright orange and pink draperies edged with scarlet.

My dear, that's our bodyguard. William is unjust about that sketch because the chalks will not make the colours bright enough, and there happened to be a short naked man on deck. They are a really fine tall set of men, and of course you remember how well they fought during the Burmese war. That must always be fresh in your memory. When we sit upon deck, one always stands so. Under all circumstances of life, we feel quite unequal to guard ourselves.

Just as we were passing today, a party of attached friends and relatives brought down a body to burn, neatly packed up in straw. The instant they got it to the water's edge, they set fire to it and sate down at a little distance, talking with great composure while their friend made a remarkably cheerful looking blaze.

November 5th. Patna.

Nobody cares about Guy Fawkes, which is odd. Emily and I actually got up at half-past-five this morning, for we anchored last night just at the entrance of Patna, and there were three miles of city to pass before we could reach the house where we were staying. The natives were gathered in hundreds, dipping their baskets of fruit in the river and then praying to them, and nothing could be more picturesque than the buildings we passed, for this is a native city.

There are about twenty Europeans in the station. We landed at half-past-eight and are most sumptuously lodged, we in the house, and tents without end pitched for all the other people out of both steamers, and furnished, too, which is very seldom done – and how any one individual has managed it in a country where shops do not grow I cannot imagine. The maids have a tent for themselves. The Lemur has arrived, but there has been a mistake about Gazelle's landing, and I am a little nervous as to how he will get through it by himself.

It is Sunday and we have been to church; that is, there is neither church nor clergyman, but the service was remarkably well done by two of the residents in the Court of Law, which on Sundays they fit up as a

chapel. Then we have been taking a drive about a very ugly country. That man on his horse is one of the magistrate's people, who was sent here to be of use in any way, upon which he has expressed his determination never to lose sight of the Governor-General. He gallops before the carriage when we drive. He has been standing through dinner today at the door of the dining room with his sword drawn, and his eyes fixed on George, as still as a statue. His next movement will probably be to go and sit at the foot of George's bed at night. I never saw so determined a bore, with a look something between Mrs Siddons as Lady Macbeth and the statue in *Don Giovanni* [see p. 67].

There have been people dining here, and I have asked pertinent questions about the station. I am fond of our host, a dark-browed melancholy looking man whose dead wife's picture is evidently hanging up in all the rooms of the house, and he himself will probably sit down and die of the trouble of us as soon as we are gone. But in the meantime he provides everybody with every possible comfort in the greatest possible way.

Good night, dear – I hear Myra ejaculating over the hard bed I am going to get into. I really believe that generally in India they stuff the mattresses with deal boards, studded with brass nails.

November 6th. Patna.

We have all been working very hard today in our several vocations. We have been visiting all the ladies of the station, breakfasting with thirty people, luncheoning with as many more. George, the misfortunate creature, has been giving audiences from ten to three and is now doing a durbar. You see that man on his camel. Man and camel have been offered to me as a present, and another man with another camel to Emily. They are part of the guard of a Rajah here. We had them sent here to sketch, and he begged we would do him the favour to accept them, and is distressed and surprised at our refusal. One Rajah is here with a solid gold howdah on his elephant, another with a silver one.

If you could but see George at this moment as I see him from my room. There he is sitting with Mr Macnaghten as interpreter. The native he is talking to prepares to have the attar of roses poured over his hands, with our servants and all his own standing behind him, some with their great silver sticks, others with their peacock's feather chouries, others with their gold embroidered punkahs, a cloud of puzzled aide-de-camps flitting about and William superintending the dressing of two old Rajahs who have had their dresses given them – one mass of gold stuff, turban, vest and tunic.

We were standing behind a screen looking at them and he told them we were there, and we had to come out for them to salaam to us. We have been all driving through the city since I wrote that. I never saw so dense a population but no fine buildings.

General Casement is low because Mrs Hawkins is staying with a friend and is lost to sight. An interest has risen about Miss Sneyd. A remarkably eligible young writer whom we meant to propose to her at Calcutta has arrived here from his station some way off, and the business looks most promising.

November 7th. Patna.

We have been passing a quiet day while George went off to the jail and an opium manufactury. William, Emily and I went after sketching the houses in the street, which are like German houses. The resemblance does not extend to the inhabitants. That is one of their carriages. The bullocks are enormous, painted in all kinds of patterns, and the horns, which sometimes extend to more than three feet, painted too.

I never told you that General Ventura dined here yesterday. Probably you do not see why I tell you now but he is an Italian who has been for twenty years with Runjeet Singh, and is supplanting General Allard in his favour. He has a longer beard and a larger emerald to clasp his velvet tunic. With great difficulty he has got leave for eighteen months to go to France, but he has been obliged to leave his daughter, who is only eight years, as a hostage, which makes him miserable. He told me, too, that though Runjeet sits in a chair himself, he and Allard have to sit on the floor cross-legged in his presence, which they dislike now other Europeans are present. The grandson whose marriage was kept so magnificently a few months ago, married three legitimate wives on the same day, which Ventura seemed to think a very natural proceeding. He talked of Runjeet having grown mean, which I believe means that he owes him, Ventura, at least three lakhs of rupees.

There's a wonderful echo near here, and there, playing to it with his flute, was Mr Beadon, the young writer. And there, listening entranced to the flute, was Miss Sneyd – pretty. The Lemur is in a peepul tree, and Gazelle bounding round it – such a touching sight.

November 8th. Patna.

George and William are gone on to Dinapore after a levee. We, being desperately attached to our host, stay on here till the evening and drive straight to the ball, which the civil and military officers are kind enough

to give us. Tomorrow we are to go to a large mess dinner, and there is a ball and supper after that, and if the day after we do not feel as if we should love society and dancing for the rest of our lives, it must be owing to the natural contradiction of human nature.

Gazelle, with great pertinacity, has kicked every native servant who has offered to lead him to Dinapore, and is going in a palanquin carriage with the maids – being rather larger than the ponies that draw it. Mrs Colvin has been not quite satisfied with the vote Mr Beadon has been giving about a fund for married people. In fact he had no business with such a vote at such a time, but we are still hopeful about Beadon.

71

November 9th. Dinapore.

On board the flat. The ball was a most successful ball last night for oh, my dear, Beadon has proposed and we are so proud of having married our only young lady. He is a nephew of Lord Heytesbury and not of age yet. George, being father generally to all the young writers, must give his consent. She is very young, too, not pretty but ladylike, and being one of a very large family was sent out to a young uncle and aunt with children of their own, and her marriage is a great thing, and when we stop three weeks hence at Allahabad it will take place. It was a great ball and a great supper, and George's health drunk with three cheers, and then ours. George had a small speech to make, of a long series all the way up the country, and we did not get on board till one, and the monster of a captain began sweeping the decks at five; and there is an inspection of the troops in the afternoon, and then a dinner of seventy-five people in the mess room. And then another ball and another supper, and I suppose I am not sleepy.

There has been a native jeweller on board with real attested authenticated jewels that are too wonderful – pearls as big as small birds' eggs. There was an emerald peacock sitting under a diamond tree, diamond pears hanging from it, that was quite too wonderful from the size of the stones. I should have bought it for you, only it cost 70,000 rupees instead of twenty pounds. There were some natives at the ball and the mere refuse of their jewels would be a fortune. At Calcutta they are all too poor to have any valuable ones. I forgot to tell you that among the presents seized after the durbar by the ruthless Macnaghten were an ivory howdah and an ivory armchair beautifully carved. The Bishop is here on the way to Calcutta.

November 11th

We have inspected and dined and balled and are now on board the flat again and I am getting to respect and revere this flat as a haven of rest. We passed a native fair this morning at Bullea and landed to see it, and Mr Torrens and Mr Macnaghten nearly fainted away on their deck because George ventured after an impromptu bit of amusement. I never saw such an orderly mob, all arranging themselves for us to pass, and the women such pictures, some with bracelets from their wrists to their shoulders. My dear, I bought myself such a beautiful set of pewter ornaments – if they would not turn black I would send them to you. No 1 is an ear ring, so is No 2, and you must pull down the rim of your ear till you make a hole large enough to put the round part of No 2 into it. No 1 has a larger round thing still. No 3 you must wear on your

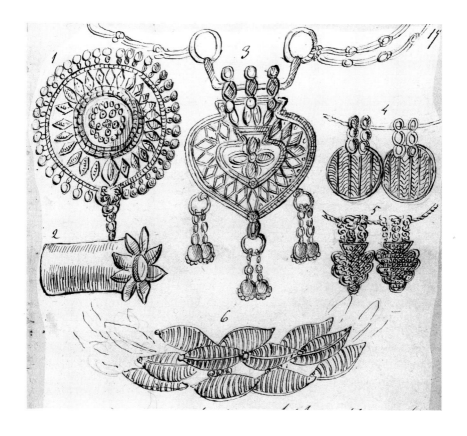

forehead, No 4 and 5 round your ankles – No 6 round your throat. That necklace is made in imitation of cowries and when I am very rich I shall have one made in gold.

November 12th. Ghazepore.
The infatuated male creatures landed again this morning on the other side of the river, to see another stud of horses, as if one stud of horses on one side of the river, was not exactly like a stud of horses on the other side of the river. But they all came back saying in the sort of tone you know, how such a horse would have suited them only it would not; and how they would have bought it only they would not. We saw Mr Torrens and Mr Macnaghten, both still overcome by our Bullea fair escapade, but there is not the slightest doubt that the precedent being now established, the next Governor-General, however old and gouty, will be

made to walk to the exact spot where we discovered we were too tired to go further.

We arrived here at two o'clock and passed a very picturesque bit of old city which we mean to go back and draw tomorrow; and at four we landed, for we are to pass two nights at a bungalow belonging to a brother of our former host. There is a beautiful garden round it and some pretty rooms, but he has made two houses into one, and our rooms are divided by such a long corridor from George's, I do not see how we are ever to see him again. Gazelle too does not quite approve of the grass here, nor the Lemur of the trees, and there are dogs about who look rude and unpolished, and they both say they would rather go aboard the flat again, so they shall go.

We have been out to drive. I wanted to go to the city to see the old buildings and they took us to Ld. Cornwallis's* tomb, that looks quite fresh from a sculptor. Then round the cantonments to look at some very respectable and, I trust, comfortable barracks. You know the sort of obliquity that makes people do that kind of thing. We saw the church lighted up as we came near and gave another shock to Mr Macnaghten's constitution by going into it without a single aide-de-camp or any other badge of a Governor-General about George. When we get into camp we mean to reform and behave better, though as it is, it seems to me we are always sailing about in a cloud of peacocks' feathers, silver sticks and golden umbrellas.

November 13th. Ghazepore.

We were taken to an opium godown and in sober earnest I have done nothing but yawn ever since. It was a curious sight – first to see there is so much opium in the world, and next that there should be consumption for it. Every year in that house there is opium worth £800,000, but it was refined barbarism in the interval between receiving visits and dressing for a great dinner and ball, and supper, to take us to see the method of preparing opium.

My dear, the process of eating dinner! The manual labour lasts 'in the Mofussil'† two whole hours, consequently for at least an hour and a half mine is purely a mental feast, chiefly shared with the Colonel or Brigadier of the prevailing regiment. I am erudite about cantonments and military hospitals and I wonder and rewonder why government does not allow verandahs to some barracks, and choppahs‡ to another. After all, though, talking is easier now than at Calcutta; there is always

* Marquess Cornwallis, Governor-General at the end of the eighteenth century.
† The provinces ‡ Thatched roofs

something in a new place to be interested about. The Bishop has been going about everywhere preaching to have steeples added to the churches. Considering there is not half enough money to keep them in repair, he might excuse the steeples.

November 14th & 15th. Benares.
We balled and supped as usual. It was a very remarkable ball owing to the extraordinary plainness – to use a light expression – of the ladies there, twenty altogether. One was pointed out with great pride as 'our only unmarried lady'; that fact was the only thing not remarkable about her. She was of that hue generally denominated orange 'tawny', in a bright strawberry pink gown. One yard wide, the sort of drawn-up features which allow a view of the back of the skull, and an embroidered bag hanging over her arm while she danced.

We slept at Mr Trotter's, embarked at eight and found ourselves at Benares at twelve. Such a beautiful city from the water, all I ever expected a native city to be. It was too early to land so we sailed the whole length of it and back again, and there was the most perfect mob of temples, no other words express the look of them rising one over the other without any kind of order, some of them half washed away by the water. The great Brahmin bulls too had their temples. The Rajah's palaces, great masses of building, were beautiful from their extreme irregularity and the masses of light and shade on them. I wrote to you from the ghaut a simple letter, sealed and sent. This was our first great landing and I will tell you all about it, then you need not ask me any more questions when we land, ever after.

Our camp was four miles from the city and crowds of natives all the way on each side of the road by way of making the horses in our carriage quite easy and comfortable. Twenty men mounted on camels with bells and harness jingling, like that one I sketched, trot on before like great mountains. Then came our own guards, then the aide-de-camps, Macintosh and Nicholson, look very well, the living images of Rosencrantz and Guildenstern. The civil Residents at a station we all look upon as very great men. I hardly like to write about them but they too go with us. When we get to the cantonments the guns begin firing and then we go through long lines of troops, the bands all taking up 'God Save the Queen' as we pass, till we arrive at the tents in a transport of loyalty about her and ourselves.

The first sight of the encampment was beautiful but I think our tents dull and grand compared to our small Rajmahal cheerful articles. They are very large, joined to George's by covered passages probably full of

75

dacoits, and we are enclosed by a large fence taking in two acres of ground and shutting out all the rest of the camp, not an elephant or camel or cooking fire to be seen. I shall take my penknife tomorrow and cut a great hole through my canvas screens which will be a heartrending scene for Byrne and Macnaghten, but nothing shall induce me to let them make a Government House of this. One comfort is William's tent is outside the compound and I shall get my sketching and a little cheerfulness there.

November 16th & 17th. Benares.
That's our tents before I get my penknife at work. We are leading such intensely busy lives just now, I am obliged to commute two days as one. Yesterday we went through the city, the most curious thing I have yet done. The streets are too narrow for carriages, so we all got upon elephants – civil authorities, Dr Drummond, Rosencrantz and Guildenstern, everybody – and as we went we could have put our heads into the upper stories on each side of us. Women were sitting there covered with ornaments and looking out of their little holes of windows, the bazaars underneath and the merchants sitting cross-legged on their stalls, the ground looking like a mass of heads.

The people throng so in these native cities, and some with their long white beards such beautiful old figures. The streets grew too narrow for elephants and we all got into tonjauns, George's of solid silver, something like a great shell. I do not know who provided it but you see him looking quite happy and natural about it. Some of the temples we went to see were very curious – such frightful gods in them, and their priests gave us garlands of flowers which they would have wished us to throw over the necks of any brahmin bulls we might happen to meet.

Today we have a great dinner to give – oh, my dear, I don't love those great dinners. The durbar tent, as it is called, has two enormous rooms in it for drawing room and dining room, which look as if they would take three weeks to build, but the tent is put up in two hours. We went on the river today to sketch the mosques. There is one mosque with two beautiful minarets which are seen at a great distance, and we all say how curious it is that there should be a mosque among those Hindu temples. My sketches will be more unassuming than ever now that we are hurried about so. I have no time. That is the next old house to the mosque [see p. 78]. There is no meaning in their buildings – an ornament is stuck over a window, one set of steps cross another, the Brahmins' shrines like coffee stalls rising out of the water, some seated in little rafts supported by bamboos with sacred lamps at the top, large straw umbrellas hung up over the walls. Some houses are an enormous height, no two alike and every one a picture.

November 18th. Benares.
George has had his durbar this morning. I went behind the screen to see him receive the Delhi Princes – twenty-four of them had private audiences. The only amusing part of the business is the extreme gravity and emphasis with which Mr Macnaghten translates every word that passes, never moving a muscle of his very unmoveable countenance. 'He says, my Lord, that your Lordship is his father and mother, his uncle and aunt, that you make his day and night, that he has no pillar to lean upon but you.' All the attar of rose ceremonies he conducts with the same solemnity. I never saw a man more born for the business.

November 19th, Sunday
We went to church today and when we came back I found a letter from you, my dearest, No. 13. I had your No. 14 a fortnight ago, but it did not turn your life the very least the wrong side out. You were at the King's illness at No. 13 and he was dead in No. 14, and by this time probably, that he ever lived is a mere Hume and Smollett* notion to you.

* Authors of the standard *History of England*.

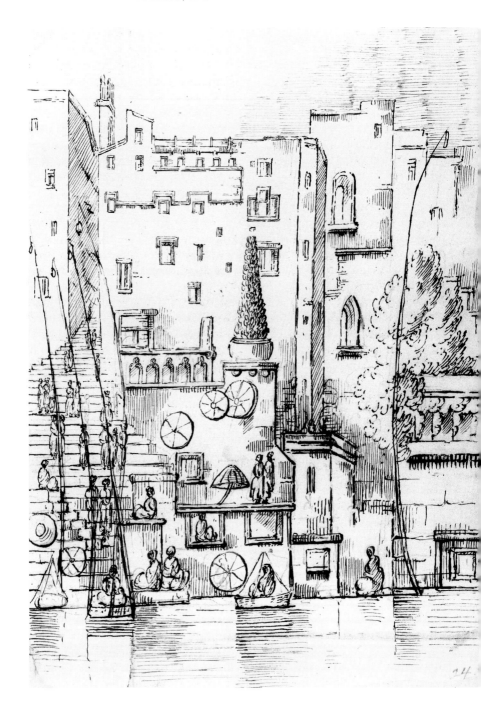

Yes, I suppose that is just what I shall be on the top of the Himalayas – you remember your sketch.* To be sure what an odd quirk it is of life to put you in Grosvenor Square and me on top of the Himalayas, when I have a heap of small remarks simmering and boiling over which only you could take the trouble to sip up.

November 20th. Benares.
We have been to see the old Delhi Ranee today. Set off at eight in the morning. The glare afterwards gets too great. We went in carriages through the city and then we set off in state. There was George in his cocked hat and dress coat, persuaded by the united mental force of all the aide-de-camps, instigated by Macnaghten and William, to mount his elephant alone, for a woman by his side would detract immensely from his dignity. The trappings of the two state elephants are quite magnificent, and what with his gold umbrella over his head, his peacock feathers and chouries, and his long train of silver sticks preceding him, he must for once have felt thoroughly happy. Emily and I were on the other state elephant, with crimson velvet umbrellas held over us and peacock feathers and silver sticks according to rule, she with a large emerald ring full of flaws on her fingers as her present to the Ranee, and I with a large gold chain remarkably light and frittery round my neck for mine; for it is the etiquette to give something we have on, and these are the kind of handsome things the Company provide by the hands of Macnaghten.

We were allowed to take all the ladies of our camp with us, and they followed on their elephants and all George's staff on theirs, and the procession was really very pretty, winding through the narrow streets. At the end of one of the very narrowest was the Palace, where the eldest son received George, who had to embrace him on both sides of the cheek, or at least make the demonstration. We were led into a little room where he and George, Emily and I were seated on little sofas. Then the prince went to a gold curtain and said the Ranee was behind. George immediately hoped, through Macnaghten, that she was in good health, and Macnaghten in the most solemn manner returned this answer: 'The Ranee, my Lord, says that it is utterly impossible for her to express how inconceivably well she feels that your Lordship has entered her dwelling.' Then the Prince got up, took Emily's hand and mine, and made some flowery speech of his mother's wish to see us, and took us behind the curtain, where we were followed by all the other ladies. One was able to interpret for us.

* Presumably in Eleanor Grosvenor's letter No 13.

She is a little old woman with magnificent eyes, most absurdly dressed in a pair of tight white trousers and net jacket quite tight, and a little white muslin draped over that. She shook our hands with both of hers, asked a number of questions: which was the eldest of the Lady Sahibs, how long we meant to remember her, how often to write to her. Her son's wife and her own married daughter, were sitting behind her, melancholy looking and not pretty, wrapped up in shawls. She said we might talk of her but not mention their names to the gentlemen. She sent for her grandchildren, who were lovely.

Then we gave our presents, and she put great diamond rings on our fingers and silver filigree necklaces round our necks, and poured attar of roses on our hands, and we took leave. Macnaghten assured George in her name that she was feeling as a locust in the presence of an elephant. He also took our diamond rings the instant we were clear of the door, which made me feel like a locust too, and we went home in the order we came, only stopping at a temple where there were hundreds of sacred monkeys, screaming and chattering and pampered to the first degree.

I am practising how to draw a camel and am not further yet in them than strait strokes and pot hooks, and they have a foolish and inconsiderate way of always waving their long throats about, which adds to my difficulties.

November 21st. Benares.
We set off at half past three this afternoon to visit the Rajah at Ramnagar, his country house, an enormous building by the side of the water. There was a nautch and fireworks, and altogether it was the most magnificent fête I have ever seen, partly from its extreme oddity and strangeness to our English feelings. The Rajah sent his boats to meet us at the other side of the river – they are made to look like gigantic peacocks swimming. On board one was a canopy with a solid silver chair for George to sit in, and on board the other two chairs were prepared for us, but we must have shocked him by giving up that boat to the other ladies, and lowering George by our presence in his. Then when we landed we found heaps of elephants prepared for us, and George was lifted up upon his silver tonjaun made in the shape of a lion and a dolphin with a golden howdah, Emily and I were one each side of him on our elephants. I happen to have a particular dislike to being on an elephant all by myself and expected the howdah would turn [over]. Then there was a mob of elephants all about us and we were taken three or four miles by torchlight. Our return, though, to the house was beautiful. They had lighted up the whole bazaar with rows of lamps and

80

the fiery outline of the old fort and temples with all the turbanned people on the top of them was very striking. All the elephants and all the attendants made a kind of rush through the gate of the fort, the torches gleaming on the camels and their riders drawn up on the other side and a remarkable quantity of eastern shew. Even the torchbearers had oil in cruets of solid silver which raised my envy from the beauty of the workmanship.

We were then taken into the house and into an enormous hall with a space between the wall and the roof where natives without end were seated to have a look at us. There was a cloth of gold laid from the door to the other end where there was a sofa and chairs up some steps. We have had to part with five servants the instant we got home, because they nearly shocked [. . .] into his grave, and I don't wonder, by scrambling for the gold cloth as fast as we took our feet off it, they having just as much right to scramble for the jewels in the Rajah's turban as any part of his property. George was put down in the middle of the sofa, Emily and I evidently as his two wives, being also allowed a seat on it on each side, and then the nautch began, and the whole scene looked like the Arabian Nights put into life. One of the two principal nautch girls was so very pretty and graceful, though nothing could be less interesting than the dance, I never grew tired of looking at her. They were covered with jewels and while they were dancing made up their long green and scarlet scarves into bunches of flowers which they glided forward and put on the steps at our feet.

We were carried off soon after to the ladies' apartments, the Rajah going with us and no other gentleman, of course. A nautch was prepared for us there – his old grandmother, mother, sisters and a heap of other women were there too. We had to kiss both cheeks of the principal of them. Mrs Macnaghten who in fact does not understand the language much acts as interpreter. O my dear, such a woman, she will be the death of me. I will say more about her when I have time. Trays of shawls and jewels were given to us, and we looked at them as if we did not see them or think them worth thanking for. We gave the old grandmother and mother rings – great diamond rings – and the Rajah gave Emily a great diamond ring with the greatest diamond pears for earrings, which I genteelly tied up in a corner of my pocket handkerchief till I could deliver them over to Mr Macnaghten.

We found George and his staff rather weary of the nautch. Our leave-taking from the old ladies had been awful, for the daughters all took a fit of fun and instead of quietly pouring attar over our hands took to smearing our gowns all over with it, laughing vehemently at the utter ruin they were perpetrating. Then came the fireworks which were good and then home which was better, but altogether it was a sight well worth seeing. I forgot to say what heaps of shawls and jewels and confectionery were brought in trays.

November 23rd. Mohun ke Serai.
I did not write yesterday because we did nothing but rest ourselves. Today I think I have done more than mortal woman ever did before in India – where one is more than usually mortal. You see, George who lives in a state of concentrated impatience at only progressing ten miles a day, settled to let the camp go its eight miles while he and I, and Rosencrantz and Guildenstern, should make a detour of thirty miles in the palanquin carriage and so see Chunar, an old fort on an old rock . . .

At six in the morning we set off that way, while Emily, Byrne and William trotted off on their elephants another. At Sultampore they had a regiment of native cavalry for us to look at. My dear, they were in light French grey uniforms. You and I could never fight in French grey. However they had good black plumes and looked well. Then we went on to Chunar, and beautiful it is. All of a sudden without any particular reason a whole ridge of hills comes in view and a great rock rising from the river and a fort full of ancient and picturesque buildings. It was an immense height to be carried up to them but the view from the flagstaff was beautiful. I cannot think how it arranged itself so in that flat country – an army was twice repulsed from that fort and I honour the fort for that. While George was doing his perambulations round the armoury and so on I sketched the bits that came in my way. That is the guard room part of the old Hindu palace. I should have sketched it better but the officer who stood by me was the very image of Liston and the sight of him made me hysterical [see pp. 84, 85].

We went to breakfast with a Captain and Mrs Stuart. Charming people. They gave us a great Scotch breakfast and then she took me to a room where there was nothing but a sofa and pillows and eau de Cologne and lavender water, and said she was sure I should like to go to sleep and she would leave me – such a model of a woman; and there were three children who like all Indian children never mind a word that is said to them. The boy would read aloud all the time George was talking, in undertones, and when they took the book away from him he read louder than ever without it. We went back to Sultampore where Captain and Mrs Smith gave us luncheon. George's head was turned by the merits of some marble cream, dug out of a quarry I suppose. I went again to lie down and Mrs Smith sate at the foot of the bed, and when her daughter left the room said, 'That poor child is married to the greatest brute in India'. I told her how sorry I was.

November 24th. Tamashabad.

Mohun ke Serai was a very good place to sleep in and that is all I can tell you about it, for after thirteen hours of society I went straight to bed. The order of the camp is that nobody leaves it before George, so that we have no dust and we start at six. This morning William and I stayed behind half an hour because we wanted to see the break-up of the camp. Five minutes after George was gone every tent was down, and for the first three miles it was all our camel guards could do to make way for us, camels restive with their loads, strings of elephants with their tents, dogs dressed up in their morning coats, palanquins, tonjauns, beds, sofas, chairs, covered carts drawn by oxen, troops, camp followers, faquirs – Mrs C. in a tonjaun, Mr C. riding by the side, Mr Wimberley driving all his family in a palanquin carriage, Genl. Casement riding by Mrs Hawkins' palanquin, Mrs Macnaghten very grand in a carriage, Macnaghten ambling on a pony before, that is now how it all is.

November 25th & 26th. Goofrein.

My dear, we are staying here for our Sunday for we always halt on Sunday, which I think right and pretty of us. The great durbar tent is arranged as a Church and Mr Wimberley reads and preaches quite beautifully, so we ought to be all very good before we arrive at Simla. I am quite taken by the Wimberley family. She speaks slow Scotch, and she lives in a state of agony because 'just as I have got a few things aboot me they are all whisked away on the back of a cammil'. And it is perfectly true, not having a double set of things, what they do possess is always on the road. To my horror, last night when William and I were

sitting outside the tent, watching with great complacency the movements of a vicious camel, it suddenly contrived to throw its load, which proved to be all the Wimberleys' stock of crockery.

I have been in great distress about Gazelle's mode of marching. For the week we were at Benares he was marched for two hours a day, being led between a goat and kid for whom he had manifested some slight affection, but he kicked them, and they butted him, and it would not do. Then it appeared that I have a cart of my own and four bullocks to

84

draw it – and he has had a house built that will go in it, between my
bookcase and armchair, and I hope Byrne does not see. The Lemur and
parrot travel with Myra in her conveyance and the interesting creatures
seem to enjoy the change of scene exceedingly.

We have the Benares Rajah following us in his tents till we are out of
his dominions, and when he has his audience to take leave, I dare say in
return for all his presents he will generously be presented with something worth 3s & 6d. His tents are rather prettily coloured. We only

came eight miles here from our last encampment and I rode most part of the way, and it was so pleasant I expect to ride a thousand miles before we stop. George will not learn to like his tent at all – he is worse than ever today, and I doat upon mine. Emily and I went this afternoon and planted ourselves and sketchbooks in the middle of the camel encampment, and they are the most impractical beasts to draw . . . Instead of following the camp in a servile manner we four are going discursing to Mirzapore. They make carpets there, you know, dear.

November 27th. Ghooper Gunj.
No, there never was such a place for sketching as Mirzapore, and I steadily set my face against going to see carpets made or anything useful done. Instead of landing with George and William, Emily and I remained in the boat and I made that masterly sketch of the Ghaut by which you were so struck, and then we went to an excellent man's house and he gave us an excellent breakfast and had an excellent lady there to do the honours to us. But, poor woman, she was the only lady in the station – there were thirty gentlemen there. She was evidently so glad to see two other women she would not cease talking. The more we told her we had got up at five in the morning and were fast asleep, the more she said 'No wonder' and talked on. She fairly talked us out into the broad sun. William drove me in a buggy (the only conveyance of the station – we all went about in buggies) to the heart of the city, and I drew a gateway to a Hindu temple. The carving in stone of the temple and native houses at Mirzapore is beautiful from its minuteness. The front of some of the houses look as if they had cut them out with small scissors, and the carpets they make there are, they say, as good as Turkey carpets, but they are not.

I never tell you anything about the country because it is generally perfectly hideous. George had not said his say nor heard his hear till four o'clock, when we set off to join the camp, having been twenty-four miles, an immense journey.

November 28th. Ghooper Gunj.
. . . There was a durbar today for the Rajah to take leave, and he came in great state with his elephants and horses and two dromedaries, which are seldom seen here. He was a clever man – there was a white cloth laid down, a sort of safeguard against his going in with his shoes on, and he wore very long pantaloons and *did* go in with his shoes on. Macnaghten and Torrens only discovered it at the end of the business, when he had

got all his presents – rather handsome ones. They both turned pale with horror to think of the misplaced white cloth. Such a pack of trash – you never saw such a way as they were in. William came away from the durbar ready to die of the pleasure of it. They rated the poor man until he said he had not an idea he was doing anything unusual, but he had, for as Torrens said, 'It is just as if I were to sit before you with my hat on my head.' 'Yes,' Macnaghten added, 'or in the presence of the King.' In the agony of the moment he forgot that the King was dead. They had nothing for it but to say, 'It was quite clear he did not know what he was doing, poor ignorant creature. It is sad to think him ignorant – they all are.'

There is no remarkable feature in this encampment beyond a paddi field and a Mango tope. We rode half the march as usual, and Gazelle has politely given William's two greyhounds two places in his carriage.

November 29th. Sydabad.
We had a long march today, twelve miles, and in consequence they made us get up at half-past-five and set off by starlight. We saw a star fall right down into a clump of trees. If Sir Isaac Newton had seen it he would have looked pretty foolish. This is what they call good en-camping ground – a great brown flat. I sketched that bit of the litter of the camp because behind Myra and the Lemur's equipage those two women were grinding grain by turning that handle. Do not you remember, 'Two women shall be grinding at one mill, the one shall be taken and the other left'? There are so many things we see here that put me in mind of what we used to call in our childhood bible pictures [see p. 88].

We met an unhappy gentleman riding, whose wife we had seen pass in a palanquin, and some of his servants, when we were encamping tonight. Thieves came into his tent last night, though he had a sen-tinel on one side. They took his uniform and all the clothes but what we met him in, except a very few which they cut up into strips. They even carried off a small camel trunk while he slept on – a camel trunk being the size of a small press. Of course we shall all be robbed and cut up this night. I have just been walking round the outside of that canvas fence they have put around us, and told William that we are not half enough sentinelled to guard our three precious persons. Such a disgraceful scene for William – when we came to his own tent we found three congregated together with three spare muskets put up. He says it was only chance, but who can believe that?

November 30th. Joosee.

Such a night have I passed. By some extraordinary fatality, all the three lights which on principle I keep burning in my tent went out. I had been told the first step of an Indian thief is to put out the lights, so I naturally concluded that all the three rooms were full of thieves. I did not dare call Myra, who sleeps upon the floor in the outer room, because nothing short of a thief stepping upon her would wake her. They took nothing because all my things are put out every night, under that scanty allowance of sentinels. But both Gazelle and the Lemur showed much signs of uneasiness and I suspect from three to six, when the sun rose, we were all three going through a series of providential escapes.

We are encamped only four miles from Alahabad but the Ganges is between us, and it will take our people two days to cross it. We went down to the river this afternoon to see the operation and a curious sight it was. The boats full of camels, and elephants swimming, and the shore strewed with all our little properties. There were eight hundred camels altogether. Those things on the backs of those elephants are the walls of the houses we live in, rolled up and going on for tomorrow, and I do not think it shews very well for George that he can want anything more solid than that [see p. 90].

December 1st. Alahabad.
That is just at the end of our encampment. It is a plausible looking temple but I suspect Alahabad is not in the least in our way – a bad flat Calcutta look about it and people driving in smart gowns, and a melancholy look-ing fort, which you and I could take as soon as look at. Mrs Macnaghten says that it is a nice sociable looking place, not dirty like Benares, and that she should like to stay here for two months. We are to immortalise it by the Sneyd and Beadon marriage. He is arrived just on the very day he ought. There never was such a man.

December 2nd. Alahabad.
William and I went into the fort yesterday evening and the intense melancholy of it was such, I was obliged to get him to make our way out of it by a short and unprecedented cut. This afternoon we went in a regular way with George to see it – a stolid man in a large cocked hat to take us through the arsenal, where there were twenty thousand guns and pistols arranged in patterns which would break a common enemy's heart to break up. Then they said they would shew us their buildings, which were eminently curious and picturesque, and the end of it was they *sot* us down, as our old American nurse used to say, to draw. I did it in bitterness of heart just to shew you what the Alahabadians call picturesque. I played an excellent trick to a great many yards of dead wall and did not leave room for them on the paper, but *that* is one old Hindu building.

The great, grand anti-Secretary plot is progressing. The old king of Oude is so infirm he cannot stand, which his subjects are by no manner of means to know, and they would know it if George were to go there and he did not rise to receive him. So Macnaghten turns pale if we talk of going to Lucknow. Then there is famine in some of the districts between Cawnpore and Agra, and so we are to be cut off from Agra till we come back again. I fancy Macnaghten and Colvin are passing many a fanciful hour composing a reason to cut us off from Runjeet Singh.

But that famine, my dear, there is something very shocking in that – the women selling their children for next to nothing and, what we think a great deal more of here, the Hindus killing and eating their sacred bullocks. They must be at the very last gasp before they would do that.

Instead of receiving visits this morning we mean to try and make ourselves pleasant to the station this evening. Coming from their solid houses into our unsophisticated tents they will find themselves pretty considerably cold, I guess. It really is cold now in the evening, when it really freezes. Living as we do in the open air we shall all be covered with white frost.

December 3rd, Sunday. Alahabad.
I like you to know what day of the week we are at. The station turned out talkative, tight sleeved and well dressed to the last degree, and the great durbar tent was allowed to suck up all the chairs and sofas from all our tents. George seemed to feel himself raised above the calibre of a kettle and three sticks under a hedge and was better. Mr Wimberley made a humble petition today for a reading desk, because as he observed to

George, though the camp medicine chest covered over looked very well, it was not quite regular.

Did not I get today your No. 16 dated July and your No. 18 dated September – one by sea and the other by land, and do not we all know how you all were and what you were all doing two months ago? Less than two months ago, for some of the papers are dated the 6th of October. I think I am disappointed about the elections. I thought the Whigs would have gained, and taking the defeats on both sides things seem to be much as they were. We have had heaps of letters and great blessings they are. It disturbs me that you had not got my Rajmahal journal. I wanted to know whether that way of writing bored you or not.

General Casement is walking up and down disconsolately because the Hawkins's have a hospitable friend who has taken them from the camp and lodged them in stone walls. I do not think that we are making half enough of Beadon; he is allowed to walk about by himself too.

December 5th. Alahabad.
There, that's a well – a remarkably clever *sketch* and utterly impossible you should understand it because nobody, not even a finished artist like myself, can draw up and down. You see I am sitting at the top of a hundred-and-thirty-two steps of which these four lines in front are some of the landing places. On the other side of this ornamented wall, there is a real round unsophisticated well, which it makes me giddy to look down, and this is one way of getting to the bottom. If George and William had any touches of human feeling about them they would be in tears at the good effect of that sketch, because now I have told you what it means you can guess they said unkind things about it all the time I was drawing. I merely want to show you that we have not any- thing, not even our wells, upon the same wretched little scale you have in England [see p. 92].

December 7th. Alahabad.
We have been doing great things in the camp today. We began by marrying the Beadons. There was something between the heartrending and the ludicrous in the business – it seemed to be such a deal to make those two young creatures promise in a tent, and there were no brides- maids. I felt too old and weatherbeaten to proffer myself, and we had to make up an altar with three chairs and some elephant hangings, and were obliged to warn them both against fainting because they and the chairs would have tumbled down. And then they were to have gone

strait off on a fortnight's voyage in a budgerow (a budgerow, you know, is a boat) which would take them back to his station. But no budgerow is to be found, so a liberal-hearted magistrate has lent them a house for two days, and then they set off travelling dak night and day in palanquins – and no servants to help them, and twenty-one years of India before them. It is a great mercy there are different ways of being happy in the world. That thought might make some people sit down and die. Not but what I am glad to see – and shall be more glad to *have* seen India – but it is fearful to think how entirely even five years will break short off our English lives . . .

December 9th. Alahabad.
. . . There is an old Begum here, the Baiza-bai is her title, whose adopted son has taken her Kingdom from her – and for a whole week the Secretaries have been in solemn and I hope wise debate as to whether we were to be allowed to go and see her. At last it was settled we were to go, but not politically. I have not the least idea what that means in India, but with infinite promptitude we agreed and said how sorry we were that we could not take Mrs Macnaghten – as of course in that case it was quite out of the question. I wonder why, and so probably did Macnaghten, but it sounded plausible and we went without her. She is by way of acting as interpreter but cannot talk Hindoostani one bit and puts horrid tactlessnesses into our mouths.

By way of doing us honour the Begum's granddaughter was sent to fetch us in her gold and scarlet-covered litter. We went in great state, and her state was an excellent parody of ours – the women running by the side of her litter with chowries, and two of them sitting astride as aide-de-camps, her state elephant painted all manner of colours and her wild looking spearmen galloping about and entirely destroying the equanimity of our bodyguard. Their nose-rings fringed with heavy pearls hurt the unfortunate riders so much that after holding them as long as they were able they finally took them out. Macnaghten translated a great many compliments between our carriages and her litter.

The Baiza-bai was a grand looking old lady without any ornaments because she is a widow. The granddaughter was covered with jewels and soon they covered us with jewels, too – emerald and diamond necklaces, pearls and diamond bracelets, rings etc. and fifteen trays of shawls for each of us were laid at our feet. They were all, I am happy to say, returned to her, as Government did not wish to receive valuable presents from her. She tried to persuade us to keep them and let her send those of less value to 'the Company'. A lady who was there as interpreter tried hard to persuade us that was the right and regular thing to do, and argued the point with considerable vehemence. William and Macnaghten and the aide-de-camps on the other side of the purdah had a nautch going on to amuse them.

Those are the King of Oude's hawks – ever so many hawkers, and cooks to cook for us while we cross his territories.

December 12th. Currah.

I have not written for two days but I am sure you will be glad to know, that having left Alahabad on the 9th we went twelve miles to Muftee, where there was nothing to see. We stayed there till Sunday, then went sixteen miles to Rupea, a sort of march that makes all the camp frantic because the horses and bullocks and tent pitchers are all tired, and Wimberley's things never come up at all. In the afternoon we all got on our elephants and went out hawking with the Oude hawk people. It was pretty from the quantity of hawkers and spearmen and greyhounds, but the murder of the birds was bad and deliberate. Today Emily and I are detached from the camp. There are a great many old Hindu ruins here and the encamping ground is four miles off, so we set off in a tent of our own, came here to breakfast, and shall join the camp in the evening . . . Their tombs run very much into temples. It is a curious place and we are going after more ruins when the sun gets low . . .

William, meaning to shoot early this morning, made a most clever and abstruse arrangement about sending his tent here yesterday and following it himself after dinner in the evening. He left us at nine o'clock when we go to bed 'in camp' and all we have heard of him since is that the Sahib did arrive and found his bed and no tent. The nights are bitterly cold now. However, there he remained on or in his bed till one in the morning, when he went on to the encampment and probably got there at three or four, for it is a wretched road and his horse was tired and had to rest when it got here. I expect to see a small row of tent pitchers' heads carefully arranged on his table today. There is something so exhilarating in the notion of nothing but a bed without curtains and one unhappy individual upon it, in the middle of these ruins.

Captain Cunningham, who is given to inscriptions and old coins, was over here just now, turning up the bricks where I was sketching. I asked him what he was looking for, expecting some erudite answer. He said, with much complacency, 'Scorpions'. At the same time I found the cast skin of a snake. I wonder where the owner is. There is a very fine old fort here, and the ground is tumbled about as if it had had to do with a well-meaning earthquake. There is about a mile-and-a-half of tombs, and I

know a battle was fought here, but whether between Mohammedans and Hindus or French and Russians I am not competent to say. 'India is so interesting from historical recollections', it is right to say, and, dearest, I am as ignorant as a beast about Indian historical recollections.

December 13th

That Oude cook* will be the death of me. He sends in about twelve dishes every day at breakfast and stands by with his satellites to see that we eat them. I happen to hold Hindoostanee cookery in horror. George tastes them all handsomely as a Governor-General should do and the old khansama always insists upon my taking some and chuckles behind his long white beard in most inhuman manner as he sees my sufferings. It was a fine moment after breakfast today when by way of a particular compliment to George, a great silver hookah was brought in with all its attendants to stand over him while he smoked it – a thing he has never even attempted. He shook his head emphatically and thereby has forever sunk us in the opinion of Oude. St Cloup, our cook, is furious at this Oude deputation. He says that un espèce d'homme came and said to him bonjour but that he could neither answer nor bow to him because he had a stiff neck and cold and that anybody can cook the bêtises he calls dishes.

There is nothing to sketch here. The evenings grow very cold now and the people all muffle themselves up in their blankets.

December 15th. Futtehpore.

I have not written for two days because the country has been so uninteresting. We are to remain there for three days and it is promising looking, very good remains of old ruins and a lovely red idol close by the camp which I must draw tomorrow.

We are expecting a young Orange Prince Henry,[†] who is in the Navy and has been sent out to see the world. He is travelling dak after us from Calcutta, which will give him a new and not very cheerful view of it, I guess. They have been delighted at Calcutta to have five days of a real royal prince though not a full-grown one. The only three newspapers existing have carried on an interesting controversy as to whether his name was William, Frederick or Henry. Byrne has been half demented finding furniture for his and his Captain's tent, and made an attack on my second dressing-table which I defended at the point of the bayonet,

* Lent to them by the King of Oude.
† a member of the Dutch Royal Family on his way to Java.

successfully. We have an enormous encampment here and a very pictur-esque one stretching for about a mile. A great many native princes with all their followers have come a long way to see us.

December 16th

There are doubts expressed as to the strict propriety of the appearance of that red idol with his head lying by him but as we have now been en-camped opposite to him for forty-eight hours and hundreds of people are generally surrounding him, my own feelings on that subject are utterly blank. He was a Ceylon God who had originally thirty-two hands and there is an interesting monkey tradition about him, how they once formed a bridge for him with their tails – the sort of thing my Lemur would show to advantage in.

Oh, my dear, that young Holland!! We fire off guns and drums at him whenever he looks out of his tent and treat him with every possible honour. He is invaluable during the Oude cook visitation, for he will eat to any amount, but of all the heavy ingenuous boys of seventeen that have ever been created, he is the most heavy and ingenuous. There is a Captain Ariens with him who speaks good English and is a pleasant man and knows people by name, and tries to throw an air of lightness over the business by saying 'Prince Harry' in a cheerful tone, and 'Prince Harry' looks up with a cheerful look and, after considerable thought, asks why the camels groan when they are loaded – the only thing that seems yet to have struck him.

There has been a durbar today and some of the followers were very striking. That man I sketched was in chain armour, and if you happen to have any stray ribbons, you can dress up your saddles so [see p. 99]. Torrens and Macnaghten are in a sad way. The Bundelkhand princes who came today give their presents as a kind of tribute and they did not give half enough – old ageing horses instead of young frisky ones and then the great man of Oude – the Rewah Raja – did not arrive in time and has been threatened with not being received at all and all kinds of horrors of that sort. But a long soothing letter in a gold bag has arrived and we only mark our sense of his conduct by making him follow on to the next encamp-ment. Still, Torrens and Macnaghten look ruffled. I personally am for conciliatory measures, for the Rewah Raja has ten thousand followers and any one of them with his long spear would run us right through the bodies. Your number 15 came today with your account of your visit to East Combe and I felt how unfair it was that you should have gone there without me. If you had only sent me a message, I would have been with you in a minute.

December 19th. Maharajpore.

We now pass through every day, the finest country for dust that it is possible to imagine and there is nothing else to be seen, not a blade of grass – the cattle are to be fed by Oude grass, just as we are to be fed by Oude cooks. We shall not pass through the distressed districts but the famine on one side of the country round Cawnpore, where we shall be the day after tomorrow, is very frightful now. A man was here the other day who had just travelled through that part and said the people were dying in hundreds by the roadside. He had sometimes seen twenty and thirty bodies lying close together. They throw aside all their prejudices of caste now and break into travellers' tents and snatch the food off the table.

Oh, my dearest! If you knew that excellent little Dutch baby we are carrying about with us, I think it would charm you. He goes into a perfect agony for himself and Ariens into another agony for him, when he has to get upon an elephant. 'Oh tell it to sit still', he said imploringly to Emily the other day, when it made a slight movement as he mounted. The Oude cooks silver some of their dishes and gild others. He is always happy when he is eating, but the deep and intellectual happiness he enjoys when he is eating rice which looks like silver, it is beyond words to express . . .

December 21st. Cawnpore.

That is one of the Caubul merchant's tents, remarkably well calculated to keep out the open air [see p. 100]. We arrived here this morning and made what is called a great entry. The excellent Dutch boy went by Emily's side in the carriage, for nothing will persuade him that it is safe to mount a horse in this country – and Ariens puts on our old nurse's frightened look for his safety if such a thing is proposed.

My white Arab is a treasure of a creature and I rode boldly in with George and his staff, charged General Oglander and his staff, stood the firing of all the great guns, rode along the lines of cavalry, and maintained that reputation for military ardour for which you and I are so remarkable in each other's estimation. Of all the ugly Indian stations I have yet seen, this is the very ugliest and dead flat, of course. But not one single blade of even brown grass to be seen, nothing but loose brown dust, which rises in clouds upon the slightest provocation. I have a notion that I really could not live here, but as other people do that may be a delusion.

We have thick carpets down in our tents now, and stoves lighted morning and evening and people here look red and coarse. They lose that delicate yellow tinge we admire so much in Bengal.

December 23rd & 24th. Cawnpore.
We have been having a busy time of it – as is always the case at these great stations. Orange is fond of dancing and instead of receiving visits in the morning we had everybody in the evening and set them all dancing and it did very well, and we told him the three ladies he danced with were of high rank and perfectly beautiful and I hope he believed us. This morning I have been very much amused by one of George's native interviews. As George cannot go to Lucknow, the King's eldest son, 'the heir apparent', Mrs Macnaghten solemnly designates him, has come here and his tents are on the other side of the Ganges. He eats with us and this morning he had his interview and a breakfast here. Yesterday afternoon four aide-de-camps went to hope he was pretty well – if three only had gone, he would have been very ill. At seven this morning four set off again to go five miles on elephants to his tents, to invite him, and he and his train of elephants which have magnificent howdahs and trappings, set off with them at eight. William

100

and Mr Colvin set off on their elephants to meet him a mile from the camp.

I went to George's room and found him putting on his very *goldest* coat, his star and ribbon and cocked hat, and in a frenzy of indignation at having to set off on an elephant, that figure, at that hour of the morning, Byrne watching him like a cat watching a mouse, and the instant his back was turned, snatching up the chair he had left him to send off to the breakfast room. George had only to go to the entrance of the encampment.

We had to assist at this durbar and at the breakfast. There are very few that ladies appear at. When the Prince got off his elephant George had to embrace him three times besides having been through the same ceremony when he took him into his howdah. The Prince of Orange had to do the same thing and we shook hands with him. I nearly made a snatch at the great emerald he had on his thumb. He is the only grand specimen of a native prince I have seen – an immense man with a good countenance . . . His turban was made of a curious combination of jewels and gold cloth, the aigrette of diamonds with two great emerald pears hanging from it. His coat and tunic absorbing a quantity of jewels too. He had two sons with him, very fair looking boys and a little rouged, some more of his family and followers, some of them rajahs who waited humbly behind his chair at breakfast.

He and George sat next to each other, flanked by Colonel Lowe as Resident at Lucknow on one side and Macnaghten in green spectacles on the other as interpreter. Orange, Emily and I sat opposite and there were fifty other people. Orange grew quite excited at the magnificence of the breakfast and wondered how such things were managed in the middle of a desert, as he was pleased to term this flourishing station. Then to my dismay Macnaghten handed me across an enormous plate of buttered rolls and said, 'The Heir Apparent expressed the delight it will give him, if you will honour him by eating these'. I looked at his sword and dagger and began immediately. Then he presented a hookah to George who was obliged to smoke it. A considerate old khansama put nothing but hot water in it but to see him and the 'Heir Apparent' puffing in each other's faces was nearly the death of me, while Macnaghten translated after this manner: 'The Heir Apparent observes, My Lord, that it is a pity your Lordship does not make a habit of so wholesome an occupation'. The Governor-General remarks he wishes not to exhaust all his pleasures at once. All the presents were then brought in and the 'Heir Apparent' looked properly disdainful.

On Tuesday we have to go and be breakfasted at his tents and on Wednesday William, Orange, Emily and I go to Colonel Lowe's at

Lucknow for three nights. I have heard I can send this off today and a friend of Mrs Drummond's will take it to England. My dearest, I have just got number 17. It is nice how your letters come. There is a great deal of trash in this and I hope it will not bore you. They have sent word that a Rajah wants to look at my Lemur and there it is, surrounded by spearmen – what a crisis! Gazelle is always excellent, but he is growing enormous and I expect him some day to murder all the native servants in a body. The parrot is out of spirits with the cold . . . Tomorrow is Christmas Day – my dearest, does it not strike you that we are little better than a set of banished men and women? However, we shall all meet again some day I hope – but I am growing very old. I am going to write to you overland for I dare say this will be long going. I shall begin another journal tomorrow. God bless you, dearest child. If this will amuse Emma and Lord Robert, let them have it.

January 1st 1838. Cawnpore.
There, dearest, I sent my first bit of journal from here a week ago, and now am beginning another year and all the last is gone without our meeting – and so will this and the next and the next and in 1841 we *ought* to be all meeting again – and *shall* we? and how shall we all feel and look and be, I wonder, and a fearful wonder that is sometimes. We are all so broken off just now, our edges will grow jagged and we shall never fit neatly in again. Keep on writing to me and do not let us lose sight of one another.

We have been for three days to Lucknow since I wrote to you last. I wrote to you the account of the breakfast that we gave Lucknow in our tents, then he gave us another in his tents, very splendid, and so like the other I need not write it all over again. But the presents he gave us – trays of shawls I am hardened about, but I have been very seriously ill ever since of a diamond and emerald fever. Oude is the greatest independent kingdom next to Runjeet Singh's, and certainly in their own way the natives are magnificent people – their magnificence running entirely to shew and precious stones. Besides fifteen trays of shawls to each of us, pearl and emerald necklaces and diamond combs, there were two sets of ear-rings, each ear-ring made of a single diamond with a single emerald drop that were too beautiful, and the presents to George were of course still more splendid. Most of them will probably be given to Runjeet Singh when we meet him. The rest of them will be sold – when I can spend a few thousand pounds for you very advantageously.

We had another breakfast at the Palace which is a very *Arabian Nights* looking building – the throne is worth £250,000 – all the pillars supporting it studded with rubies and the fringes round the canopy pearls and emeralds . . .

In the evening we had to go to the Palace again to see some fireworks. Nobody but ourselves, Macnaghten who came over to act ambassador, Col. Lowe at whose house we were staying, the Orange baby, the Oude family (for 'Oude and we are very familiar') and about eighteen brothers of them and sons in proportion, all remarkably happy in the shape of their turbans. There was written up in letters of fire 'God save Lord Auckland Governor General of India', 'God save the King of Oude and Col. John Lowe resident of Lucknow'. I was particularly taken by the sublimity of that . . . But it was altogether a striking looking scene, the banks of the river were illuminated, the fire works were let off from the water and boats full of nautch girls and jugglers in their splendid dresses were lighted up in front.

We went next day to see some of the King's garden palaces. One is beautiful, of inlaid marble, fountains playing in all the rooms and the garden full of flowers – orange trees covered with ripe oranges and parroquets flying about in flocks. The ladies' apartments are always melancholy-looking – built up by high walls . . . The city is full of beautiful mosques and buildings. One of the palaces we saw had just been pulled down and rebuilt because one of the last King's three hundred wives had died there – another had poisoned herself finding he had grown tired of her. He was only 35 years old when he died this year and seems to have been quite mad from folly.

Having the power of life and death over his subjects it happily did not take the turn of extreme cruelty. He only now and then put them in prison without any reason and took their property to help on one of his own whims. His chief amusement was dressing, and I saw an excellent sketch, not of him but of his train, done by a native. He heard that our Kings wore long trains at their coronations and so he had one made for himself, so long it extended through two or three rooms. There is a sketch he had done of the finest room in his palace with a long file of servants passing through it bearing part of his train, neither the end of it nor he himself appearing. When the Bishop was there he took a great fancy to his dress and suggested that he should make one like it. Think of the Bishop's horror. The English hair dresser he had taken into his service was in despair because at the King's death he was left in possession of eighteen wigs of different colours which the King had ordered for his own wear at one hundred guineas each.

There is one palace called the egg palace which looks at a distance exactly like a great white egg – he had it built because he wanted something peculiar. I did that from a native sketch of him in one of his

carriages. We met there a Captain Patten who is a great Thug fancier – has a prison full of them and makes positive pets of some. He wanted us to go and see them and the gentlemen did go and see a regular Thug exhibition. They show how they follow their victim, how they sometimes stupify him and their various modes of strangling him. It is a foolish exhibition and once, they warmed into the play so much, they nearly strangled a sepoy in good earnest. He had some horrible drawings and models of the whole process and Emily has sent some he offered to Ld. F. Egerton. So you may be thoroughly enlightened. We passed through a village where eleven hunded of their victims were buried – there was a man there who had been present at four hundred murders. . . . We lost our Orange baby there – he and Captain Ariens went on to Delhi. He never passed a happier time – there was a great deal of native eating to do there, as well as English, and he laboured hard in both occupations. People breakfasted too at different hours and he breakfasted

104

with them all. Upon the whole we rather miss his little taking infantile ways and William came home declaring he felt like a mother who had sent her child to England.

The Oude prime minister died suddenly the day before we went there, a clever old man of eighty, and we were all as consternated as if he were an English prime minister and said how hard upon the old King – and I wondered who would come next. I listened to all Col. Lowe had to say about it and think upon the whole I was interested. I have a great respect for Oude – there seems to be something like politics there, but on a narrow scale, for the King would naturally cut off the head of a formidable opposition. Sir Charles Metcalfe* is here on his way to England.

January 3rd
I have been doing some Oude people's head-dresses – we have a great many of them with us still – and all the cheetahs in case we like to go out hunting with them. I keep that concealed from Gazelle in case it should hurt his feelings and give him disturbed nights. That man with the gun has a brass cap. They are a fine looking set of guards [see p. 107].

My dearest, I am sick at heart with all this starvation we see about us. Now we are only upon the outskirts of the country where famine is raging but we are among those who have only wandered from it to die, and even here some of the villages are depopulated, the crops are dying fast for want of rain. As yet there are funds at all the civil stations for giving food to all who want it but many die upon the road and every day we see those who do not seem to have an hour's life left in them. Every evening all who come are fed with rice but even these were more than three hundred and it was found difficult to prevent them tearing the rice from each other. Some scarcely look human, particularly the children. It made me shudder yesterday to see one little wretch who was lying alone in the middle of the camp tear bread off the loaf with his teeth which it had hardly strength enough to swallow. The mothers offer to sell their skeletons of babies for a rupee. The fathers seem to get what food they can for themselves and to leave women and children to starve – but many men too quietly lie down and die. If rain would come during the next fortnight, the crops for the next year might be saved and then the rich natives who have grain in their granaries might sell it, but it is generally during the Xmas week that the rain comes and there is no appearance of it. Already I feel as if we were only giving a few more days

* He had been provisional Governor-General between Lord William Bentinck and Lord Auckland.

of misery to those we feed, for they must die of hunger at last. Three or four days will take us away from the sight of all this suffering but I am sure I will never forget it.

We are rather oppressed just now, by a lady, Mrs Parkes,* who insists on belonging to our camp and has entirely succeeded in proving that the Governor-General's power is but a name. She has a husband who always goes mad in the cold season, so she says it is due to herself to leave him and travel about. She has been a beauty and has the remains of it and is abundantly fat and lively. At Benares, where we fell in with her, she informed us she was an independent woman and was going to travel to Simla by herself – which sounded very independent indeed. Then she applied to Captain Codrington who manages the ground to let her pitch her tent among ours. Now the sacredness of the Governor-General's street of tents is such that . . . of course that was refused. The Magistrate of one station always travels on with us to the next. To each of these Magistrates she has severally attached herself, every one declaring they will have nothing to do with her, upon which George observes with much complacency, 'Now we have got rid of our Mrs Parkes' – and the next morning there she is, the mawk, her fresh victim driving her in a tilbury – and her tent pitched close to his. William knew her a little when he was in India before and she plies him with constant notes and small presents. We are longing for the day when we shall find him conducting her on the march. That is one of the howdahs belonging to the Oude elephants which are still with us. The canopy is made of silver embossed [see p. 108].

January 7th. Kanonze.
I have not really had the heart to write the last three days – we have been surrounded by people dying of starvation. Some hundred came for food yesterday, a thousand were fed today, but many of them are still lying round the camp, children who have not many hours of life left in them – some of the grown-up people too are nothing but skin and bone, their faces like skulls. Captain Cunningham found many more today, one woman dead and a man and woman dying, many sitting round but taking no notice. There is plenty of grain too in the granaries but the rich natives, from fear of a greater scarcity next year, will not sell it. The distribution of food is grown very difficult, they will not wait for their turns but rush forwards to tear it from each other and the children are nearly crushed. Almost all our native servants have adopted either

* Fanny Parkes, author of *Wanderings of a Pilgrim in Search of the Picturesque* (1850). An indefatigable linguist, traveller, and collector of information.

orphans or children they have bought for a rupee or two – a very common thing in these times of distress – and they generally keep them for the rest of their lives. We are now within three days of Futteghar and there work is provided for all who can work and funds to support the women and children who cannot. We think we must lose Mrs Parkes tomorrow, for Mr Bose, a thin, unhappy-looking Magistrate, has been to beg Captain Codrington to conceal where his tent is to be pitched as he is very much worn out attending to Mrs Parkes. William had a note complaining that her 'little wrist strap' was stole and wanting to know where to go for redress.

January 9th

Our poor people are improving a little and have been much less vociferous today. I saw a gentleman today who has come from that part of
the country from which these have wandered, and he says the sights
there are horrible – hundreds dead and he saw many as he passed strip-
ping bark off the trees and cooking it. Our French servant went out to
look for canteloupes by the side of the river, and found above a hundred
lying together and some skeletons upright in the water, and passed
through a village where but two inhabitants were left. My dearest, I am
longing to be away from all these horrors, where I feel that we can do
but little good – all that is consumed by man and beast comes to us from
Oude. The country is bare even of grass – at the best it is thinly inhabited. But it is no affectation to say that when we sit down to dinner
with the band playing and all the pomp and circumstances of life about
us, which is just as much kept up in a tent as anywhere else, my very soul
sickens at the cries of the starving children outside which never seem to
cease.

You will be glad to know that when George and I were walking to
warm ourselves after our ride we came upon a little tent just outside the
line of sentinels. We wondered who it was and about twenty voices
answered: 'Bibi Parkes!' This has been a heavy blow.

January 10th. Futtepore.

There is appertaining to our camp a little man on a little white horse
who wears a little red tunic and a little red turban – it his business to
ride before George wherever he may go, whatever conveyance we are in
or on. The little man and horse are seen a hundred yards before us –
their pace never seems to change. He is called Sancho and is exactly
Sancho Panza in look, and that sketch is of his father, who is now
between eighty and ninety and who also bore the name of Sancho, when
he ambled on before a successive number of Governor-Generals and
Commanders-in-chief [see p. 111]. His real name is Kurif Singh, but he
told us today that he and his family preferred the name of Sancho who,
he understood, was a great warrior. William knew him when he was
with the Amhersts, and the old man brought all the little Sanchos to the
fourth generation to see him, and our Sancho stood by with an air of
filial submission while he descanted on the merits of them all, and he
actually insisted on having his picture drawn because he said all
Governor-Generals wished for his picture. I sketch figures now in the
most intrepid manner considering I cannot sketch them at all.

There is much less distress about us here though some dreadful individual instances of it. All those who have followed us will have work given them or be taken into the asylum. I am sure you will be pleased to know that yesterday as we were returning from seeing some ruins, George said, 'There comes Macintosh (Rosencrantz) and Colvin on an elephant. How fat Colvin grows.' 'Colvin' turned into Mrs Parkes in a man's hat and riding habit. She had met Captain Macintosh and as far as we can make out had climbed up the elephant's tail into his howdah when least expected. She will certainly be the death of us all. Gazelle persists in knocking down all the chimneys of all the stoves. He will break my heart and burn us all on our sofas.

January 12th. Futtepore.
We are still here because George has had a durbar and we had all the station one evening, consisting of seven ladies. When we do go into the army, dear, we will form a troop of irregular horse – we have some with us now and I never saw such grand looking articles. They wear what uniform they please and cover themselves with gold embroidery upon their tunics. Three of them walked in for orders when William was with me and then came strait up to me and offered me their sheathed swords. I was exceedingly puzzled what to do with them, being totally unused to fight with three swords at once. However, with wonderful instinct, I majestically touched each of them, at which evolution William looked relieved.

There is a Major Sutherland staying here now, who commanded some of the Nizam's people and when he left them they gave him a sword, and the sheath to that sword was the prettiest thing that ever was composed – a mass of large turquoises and small diamonds. If ever there should be a Mrs S. she will probably wear it herself. I cannot think where all the precious stones come from in this country. I look about at every fresh encampment and never pick up any.

A man – a magistrate – a monster – took us through six miles of deep sand to look at that frightful ghaut on the other side.

January 14th
We have crossed the river and are in Rohilcand. That fact at once makes our position familiar to you. Many a good hour have we passed in Grosvenor Square smoking . . . and talking over Rohilcand – this familiar recollection brings tears into my eyes.

I have this moment got a letter from you, dearest – your Bowood one, No 19 – not three months old. You mention having got one of mine,

and talk about Ludlow and Smith, which is so very – it actually brings us together. Gazelle lies upon a shawl still. Chance growls and eats plumb cake. Fairy is bringing up her fifth family. I hope that boy you 'placed out' may continue to do well but I have my doubts – he will eat too many roasted potatoes or do something heinous. I am sure I am the last person to wish to judge you severely – but looking at the whole story impartially, from this distance, I cannot say I think you came very well out of that child's leg business. I have thought for some time that there are two or three of your poor girls quite unaccounted for. However, as neither Lord Grosvenor nor the laws of your country say anything I shall not. I see Bowood just as you describe it. The furniture there was always prettier and comfortabler than anywhere else, and I do not suppose that Mr Smith can have anything to do but to frank your letters to me and I am sure he does it very well.

We are in a very prosperous looking country now. The moment we crossed the river we seemed to leave all distress behind us. The crops here are green and flourishing and we all look like pigmies compared to the size of people we meet. The Rohilcandians are evidently remnants of the giants mentioned in the Bible and I expect they will step on all our poor little Bengalees and crush them. They have a great quantity of shawl drapery about them and fine turbans and are altogether most imposing looking articles.

I am in a sad way – I cannot get any fruit for the lemur, Rolla. It is very odd I never thought of telling you his name before. When guavas failed he condescendingly consented to eat the apples the Persian merchants bring, and now he has got to his last apple and the old khansama and I 'weep as we think of the morrow'. A philanthropic magistrate the other day sent an express thirty miles who returned with six guavas. That man ought to be rewarded. William has entrapped the Governor-General into his tilbury and carried him off out shooting. I dread Macnaghten's rebuking eye. It is curious but he always keeps one eye shut.

January 16th. Futteygunge.
I never saw such a country as this. There is nothing to sketch but I have got six apples. A poor man who had procured them with great difficulty because he was going to give a dinner thought it his duty to offer them to Rolla, who instantly closed his black hand upon one and ordered the others to be saved.

Emily had ten rupees taken off her table two days ago and Byrne has been making her servants try the rice trial to know who is the thief.

William, upon the mere threat of such a thing to his servants, had a valuable watch put back upon his table which had been stolen. The native who conducts the trial gets what they consider a sacred rupee and the weight of that rupee in rice is given to each of the suspected people. And then they chew it and spit it out (not quite nice) but the thief never can succeed in chewing it. It comes out of his mouth dry and just as he put it in. I was sitting in Emily's tent just now when Byrne walked in with much majesty and declared the thief was found and pointed to one of her very best servants who had been fifteen years at Government House. The trial has evidently failed, which it seldom does, for the real thief generally confesses from nervousness. This man has been long trusted in various ways and is not the least likely to have stolen anything, but most of the others will firmly believe he has, though he declares he has not and it is only as a subject for forgiveness that he can be kept. William asked Ariffe confidentially what he thought of the business, as my servants had nothing to do with it – to which he answered with an air of superiority: 'I not think much of that trial. The man is a good man, no thief, but he a fretting frightened man, so his throat dry. We don't all believe in those things.'

My dear, I see an old gateway in the distance and am going to sketch it. I have been drawing the chief of our irregular horsemen [see p. 115]. They are such a grand looking set of creatures – when they stalk into William's tent with their offerings of flowers and vegetables they look like so many living melodramas. That one wears Runjeet Singh's plumes tipped with gold on his own and his horse's head. He has thick chouries hanging to his saddle cloth and his legs are buried in them. They are a defence against sabre cuts. He has two followers with long lances but I had no room to sketch them. This one's dress and his saddle cloth are covered with silver embroidery. And now in utter desperation as to finding anything else I am going after that old gateway. A battle was fought near it – I wonder when, and with whom – don't you?

January 19th. Bareilly

I have been trying to do that giant in armour, who went to the Magistrate and said he was sure we should like to do his picture [see p. 117].*
I never saw a more enormous mass of conceit and if I were the horse I would break down with him. He is a great character in his way, has a pension, calls himself Colonel, comes to the durbar, covers his horse with necklaces and himself with chain armour. That . . . thing in front is

* Under the picture is added: 'This man was hung a year after for beating his wife's brains out.'

to cover his nose when he fights. I like our irregular horsemen much better than him. They did their exercise for us the day after we left Futteygunge. Off their horses they stalk about with a 'I-have-discovered-the-secret-mine' sort of look about them. On horseback, tilting with their long spears, riding full gallop at tent pegs and carrying them off, fighting with single-stick, charging with the Mahratta war cry, they have a grand wild effect which is taking. On two pounds a month they keep themselves and their horses, but the richer among them, like the one I sketched, have generally three or four poor relations in the corps, who serve him as esquires, and get their pay by clubbing together . . .

This man came with a detachment to greet us, and when he rejoined his officers and the rest of his company here, the others embraced and congratulated him upon having done honour to them, as the Lord Sahib had given him spears for tilting before him, and the Lady Sahibs had drawn his picture. He sends us nosegays every morning, which fact, coupled with their embroidered dresses, determines me when I take the field to command the irregular horse.

We were met today two miles from the encampment by Brigadier Tombs. I thought you would like to know that we know a Brigadier Tombs, for it is not everybody who does. We are civilly huffy with him because he moved our encampment, because he said it was encroaching on his parade ground. If it had been a churchyard he would have had reason to complain.

We are going to receive all the station this evening. We have lost Mrs Parkes. One unhappy day she encamped actually in our lines, which threw the military authority into an agony of fuss. Captain Codrington went and civilly insinuated she must not do that, and had better follow with the regiment, to which she replied that if she did not go with our camp she would not follow at all, to which no reply was made, and we have never seen her since.

Rolla has had a basket of pears sent to him, each pear wrapped up in cotton, because they come from a far-off country, and he has made Gazelle a present of his plantains which he was trying to eat for want of something better.

January 21st
George has been having a durbar, and that is the carriage one of the Rajahs came in – the body of an English barouche mounted on high wheels and two great elephants to draw it. The Rajah it belongs to is supposed to be rather in the free-booter line. Macnaghten uses a very

emphatic shake of the head when he speaks of him and I overheard all kinds of precaution being taken to have his shoes off in time. At all events he has a good taste in carriages, as you can see. There were two small elephants trotting on before with saddles on their backs.

That is a striking likeness of William, smoking his hookah and suffering under what he calls a fit of the Bareillies. I did it while I was trying as usual to prove that he and George have no right to grumble about anything, because they are paid for what they do, and Emily and I, the great unpaid, are the only people to be pitied, and they should not let their faces grow twice the usual length of human faces when ours keep their natural shapes. If that sketch does not serve as a warning I do not know what will [see p. 119].

This evening, too, we are to do a bit of extra duty. We received all the station yesterday evening and made them dance and it went very well. Today George gives a dinner to fifty men and we meant to have rested

117

on our oars. They have settled that we, two helpless females, are to assist, which is hard. I shan't say much to Tombs.

A deputation of natives has been to Captain Nicholson to ask for his black monkey with a white face, that they may carry it to their temple for a few hours and worship it. They saw it sitting at the door of his tent and it was a new species of idol to them. The Monkey is gone off in state with his own bearer to carry him and it will turn his head with vanity. I fear the same thing should happen to Rolla – he shall never appear at the door of his tent without a veil. He is vain enough already.

We have been out to drive, and as usual there is nothing but a great dusty plain without a blade of grass.

January 23rd. Futteygunge.
It is a little hard to fall in with two Futteygunges in one journey, and what I never expected. It almost looks as if we were going backwards. We left Bareilly this morning. Nothing could be . . . than that long dinner at which I've assisted. I sate next the head of the civil service there, a real proud position, and meaning to make an effort to find a suitable and intellectual topic, I said something about an old Mrs Grant, who is past eighty, being a wonderful woman. To which he replied as if he thought her young and flighty, 'But her mother, ma'am, you probably recollect her – she was a charming woman. You don't happen, ma'am, to recollect her maiden name?' Now he has put it in my head, I suspect I am a contemporary of old Mrs Grant's mother before she married . . .

January 24th. Kamera Dam.
. . . I have been reading a great many examinations of different Thugs, and upon the whole they are certainly an interesting people. But the more I read about them the more persuaded I am that we are entirely surrounded by them. Ariffe is missing at the moment, and I daresay has gone to worship Bowhanee, goddess of destruction. I see that one who is asked why they stab the dead bodies says: 'That Bowhanee may have blood – Bowhanee delights in blood'. One man 30 years old speaks of having strangled 120 with his own hand and to have been present at the murders of 400 or 500. They deny with the greatest indignation the idea of being thieves, and the question always seems to draw down a storm of indignation on anybody who asks it. There is one remarkable old Thug of 65, winds up his answer in this way: 'If I got a farthing by Thuggee I would take it but never by theft. A thief! No, he is a contemptible being, skulking thus' – he imitated a skulking thief – 'But a Thug' –

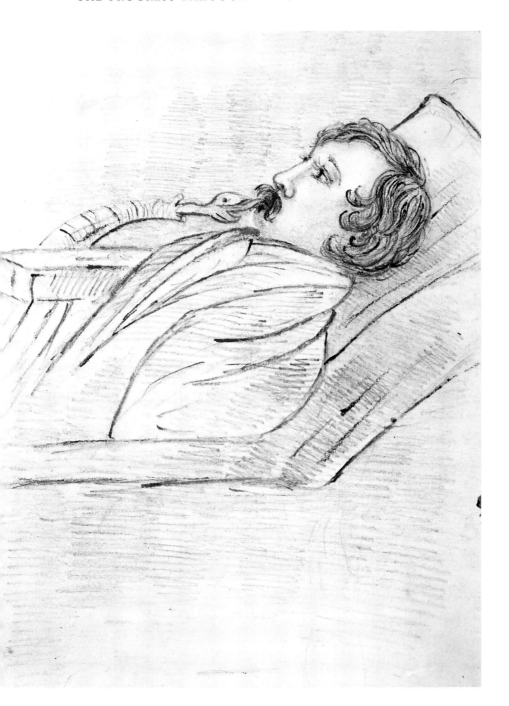

rising with animation – 'wears a dagger and shews a front. Thieving – never! If a banker's treasure were before me, entrusted to my care, though hungry and dying I would scorn to take it. But let the banker go on a journey I would certainly murder him. I despise a dacoit, a robber! Let him come before me!' Such a highly moral sentiment, and I observe that all the Europeans who have had much to do with their examinations view them in a most romantic light, and look upon those who are hanged almost as martyrs.

We are in the Rajah of Rampore's territories, and the servants who move with the camp, that goes on the night before us, are in an agony of terror, and all set off in a body with the guard for there is an idea, and a true one, that he encourages his subjects to rob, and will put up with a little murder. He came to the durbar with that elephant carriage, and George went yesterday to his palace and says the crowd assembled was the most picturesque he has seen – the house tops covered with women, which is not usual. One of them called out that now they had got hold of the Governor-General they had better keep him. I wonder what we should have done if they had carried on that idea. Emily and I must have marched at the head of Wright and Jones to the rescue, and Mrs Macaghten, who always knows what we do, would have followed with her ayah. There were only women left in the camp . . .

It is a most interesting country just now. George has adopted a pariah dog for his own pet – it has followed us for two months. We call it the Honourable John, in compliment to the Company.*

January 27th. Moradabad.
There are the whole range of the hills in view, and many peaks behind them – such a satisfactory sight. It proves there really are hills in India, which after a thousand miles of uninterrupted plain I had begun to doubt. It is very cold, too; the thermometer has been at 33 the last three mornings when we started. It has been a heavy march this morning and a river to cross, and there is wailing in the camp for the carts stuck in the sand. As usual Mr Wimberley and his innocent family were found pushing at the hind wheel of their own carriage, and at last borrowed an elephant to drag it out, to the elephant's infinite disgust. As usual George pursued his impetuous course through the water of a most dangerous ford, and his habit got horridly wet, and I was splashed all over by his and William's horses and there was a dangerous cataract behind us of aide-de-camps, Secretaries, guards and camels and much irregular horse. It might have been my last hour, only it was not. Emily's

* The Honourable East India Company

carriage horses grew restive when she was coming through the city, and she had to walk a mile and a half with the two European servants and their riding whips on each side of her – a most august sight.

Captain Patten has sent six sketches of Thugs acting their little innocent transactions with travellers, and I will copy them, though the last makes me rather sick [see pp. 122, 123]. This is a very neat little station, only four ladies and two sickly.

January 29th. Moradabad.

We have not moved yet because of Sunday and today George has a durbar. The Rajah of Rampore has sent a man to take the pattern of his dress coat, so I hope he is going to have one like it – it will be nice to see them dressed like brothers and will delight the hearts of Macnaghten and Torrens.

Such a catastrophe befell me this morning. I heard a suspicious crackling and looked out and saw one side of the tent in flames, I being comfortably in bed. They had overheated the stove in my sitting room and that was the result. The noise that followed alarmed the whole camp. About a hundred native servants screaming fire and water – the ayah sobbing and moaning, the European servants rushing out strait from their beds, the sentinels astonished and severe, and the conduct of the Hon. John above praise for he rushed howling to my bedside. I believe the fire was stunned for it was got under in two minutes, just as I was thinking of making a dignified retreat with Gazelle and the Lemur. Luckily the walls of a tent are not so long rebuilding as those of a house.

The hills look beautiful this morning. I wonder if we shall know how to balance ourselves on top of a hill – probably we shall all tumble down. As there is nothing to sketch I go on copying those Thug sketches and they make me feel Thuggish.

January 31st

The roads grow worse every morning, and the names of the places we stop at more unpronounceable. Captain Codrington goes on every night to pitch the camp and sends back an account of the road written by his sergeant, that we may arrange our travelling plans. Every day his view of our prospects grows more gloomy. This is tomorrow's: '1st mile – ruff and dusty (he evidently thinks ruff a more emphatic mode of spelling) 2nd 3rd and 4th mile rugged and sandy, 5th mile a brute no water, very bad passage – better go on the left of it; and 6th 7th and 8th miles, very rugged and heavy, 9th, 10th and 11th miles, better but ruff and dusty –

Thugs fixing the attention of a traveller upon something mysterious in the clouds, that he may be strangled unawares.

Thugs in the act of strangling a traveller.

Thugs strangling a traveller on horseback.

(I left a space for another Thug drawing, but when I found that they came to the stage of stabbing their victims' eyes before they threw the bodies into the well, it would be sickening employment to follow them further into the mysteries of their trade.)

123

Camp 11 miles distant by perambulator – encamping ground dusty and not good.' This is the sort of bulletin that carries desolation to Wimberley's heart and makes him assemble his family round his palanquin carriage to weep over it. In the morning he is seen in the dim light before sunrise walking before it, pointing out to the coachman where the ruts are the least deep, then getting on his grey pony to amble a little more. Then in deep distrust of the coachman, mounting the box to drive. Another touching sight on the road is old General Casement walking up and down by his tilbury watching for a distant sight of Mrs Hawkins's palanquin, that he might persuade her to let him drive her for the remainder of the way.

There are some animal objects of great interest that we pass. These are a cow, a goat and a white poodle, belonging to a man who generally rides the cow, and every morning now for near a thousand miles we have passed them on the road. If a strange dog looks at the cow the poodle bites the dog and licks the cow's nose to comfort her. The black goat he never allows to stir from his side. Yesterday we saw them all progressing in a very slow manner and then it appeared the black goat had produced two black kids, and the poodle was paying them the most delicate attention.

Young camels of two or three days old are the strangest sights. Their bodies and the length of their legs so utterly out of proportion they look as if they were mounted upon stilts. There *was* a young buffalo of much promise whose first faltering steps we had watched. He wore a scarlet petticoat and supported the fatigues of the march for three weeks. One miserable morning we saw its dead body on the road. The next, the maternal buffalo was carrying its skin, but over this scene I must drop a veil.

February 1st. Amrora.
We are encamped today near what was a great city, and it is still thinly inhabited by descendants of the original possessors of it, and they naturally consider it their own. They have the character of being the greatest ruffians in India, but are remarkably happy in the shape of their turbans. They burn villages and massacre the inhabitants. Still, there is a redeeming point in the folds of their yellow cashmere . . .

George is growing rabid with his tent life and scolds me every morning because the country is not prettier.

This afternoon William and I found rather an imposing hill of sand with a tomb on the top, which I sketched, and a view from it of the old city and mosques scattered about, altogether rather impressive. I sent word to George that he had better come, and he did, and was more rabid than ever because he had been half way up his ankles in sand and would not own that the view was a view.

February 2nd
I did that gateway at Moradabad, and of course you will be sadly puzzled to find it after Amrora. I was so hurried I could not find my way in the book, and then it turned out to be the entrance to a native's house, who came out with beads in one hand and rupees in the other, that we might touch them [see p. 126].

There is an alarm in the camp that the weather is going to grow hot much sooner than it ought, owing to the want of rain, in which case we shall be in a scrape before we get to Simla in April. We are now within four marches of Meerut, and an awful phalanx of balls and parties are rising up before us there. I am contemplating a most distressing parting there with Gazelle. Captain Champneys is settled there and will take charge of him while we are in the hills. No cart or carriage can go further than the foot of them, and all sorts of dangers await him there in the shape of leopards and wild dogs, and so he must have an asylum provided for him. But I shall miss him dreadfully.

February 4th
No ships came and consequently no letters and that disturbs me. Our latest sea letters are six months old. How very disgusting. That man is a pilgrim who has travelled about a thousand miles at the rate of ten or fifteen miles a day to fill his baskets with holy water. It seems to me that they always consider that part of the Ganges which is farthest from their homes as the holiest [see p. 127].

Captain Nicholson caught up two yesterday and brought them to be sketched. One of them refused to take money, but the other, who was a brahmin, said he should apply it to a holy purpose and carried off both shares. I was just now reading in a translation of a kind of native newspaper some of Runjeet Singh's summary Bow Street ways: 'The Maharajah finding him to be a murderer judged him to be hanged. The Maharajah found him a thief and sent him to prison.' It is seldom he puts anybody to death – the forfeiture of a limb is a much more common punishment. Some men for repeated offences have had both hands and both feet cut off and then their eyes put out – but he is not reckoned cruel.

A large army of civil powers and one civil power's wife came out to

meet us here. I do not see why George should not take on like a Maha-rajah and turn magistrate for himself.

February 6th. Meerut.
There, I am sure it will be a pleasure to you to think of us in what is called the best station in India – George doing his levee, we going to receive all our white fellow creatures in the evening, seven days *rest* before us, to be rendered piquant by three great dinners, three balls and suppers and one amateur play.

By far the most amusing incident I have seen took place this morning. We were riding in, in great state, through the lines of the line regiment, about sixty of the reigning Meerut princes round us, when one of the private's horses threw its rider, dashed in among us, and for a wonder not being vicious, took a line of its own and was engagingly playful. Its first attack was upon the advanced guard in the shape of Sancho and his pony. He stood opposite to them on his hind legs and Sancho, evidently dreading the descent, quietly rolled off on the other side. Then he ran right into the midst of us, singled out dear old Macnaghten, who made his horse turn round and round in a figure of eight as well as any native could do it. I never saw a better chase. Next he piaffed up to Captain

127

Codrington, who followed Sancho's example and threw himself off on the other side. Then he dashed at us. George, William and I with great presence of mind rallied round ourselves. The General, who had rode out to meet us, fenced with his stick. Emily, who was in the carriage behind, was overcome by the sublimity of the scene. In India it is reckoned as easy to seize a loose tiger as a loose horse.

February 8th. Meerut.
There are two old faquirs who always follow the camp and plant their flag a mile from it. There they sit beating their drums to show that the camp is near, and a very cheerful sound it is to the marching people. I sketched one of them this morning with the bullock he rides behind him. He always sings a remarkable loud song as we pass, 'In Honour of the Lord Sahib, my prince'.

Upon the whole I do think this place is more calculated for human creatures to live in than any other I have seen in this flat desert they are pleased to call a country. The gardens are full of flowers and fruit trees in blossom, and even this year when there has been no rain, there is appearance of green grass. The houses, too, are pretty looking and if people do happen to like each other, there are greater numbers of them here to like.

William's old regiment, the 16th Lancers, are here – it has been here all the time he has been in England, and will only make a semblance of going home again three years hence, for hardly any of the men who came out in it are left. Emily and I the other evening went into the burial ground which is near the camp. Here they put large monuments over the graves of Europeans of all classes, and they cover a large space with broad gravel walks running among them. It is really true that among the hundred we passed we found but one person who had lived to the age of 50. Most had died under 20, or between 20 and 30, and that is the case in most Indian burial grounds. We have done two balls and one dinner.

February 10th. Meerut.
I sketched that man with his cross-bow today [see p. 131], and I have been to Captain Champneys to see Gazelle's future habitation, and he will have a large park, but it goes to my heart to part with him. He is such a handsome looking old thing, at this moment lying on the carpet and fonder of me than ever. I believe I would let him brave the leopard and hyena demons if I did not live in dread that he would run his horns through

some of the native servants – he takes such dislikes to some – and a tame deer is then very dangerous. But Ariffe has been to say 'they think it great pity of Ladysheep to send him then away, he only makes very pretty play'. Rolla looks as if the approaching parting hurts his feelings. There is a native painter here. I made George sit to him and the sketch he has done of him is supposed to be the best likeness that has ever been achieved. It is surprisingly clever. Emily has got one of William from him that is very successful too. I suspect the natives are much cleverer than we are.

February 12th. Meerut.
Three balls now, but they are well managed and end early, and all the people dance hard, as if they like it, and so it all goes very well. I do not think I have ever told you enough about what we eat. In this part of the country there is every vegetable that ever was invented, and oranges and pomegranates and grapes, and in the right season strawberries, and then come pears and apples that come from a distance, wrapped up in cotton and tasting like turnips. They took us in in England, when they talked about the quantities of curry we were to eat. The natives eat it but I hardly ever see Europeans touch it. They roast innocent kids and call them lamb; that I detected for myself. I wonder nobody has thought of eating a young camel. They look tender and good. The last time we marched I saw a camel with two little ones running along and carrying a third on its back, such a blow for the father camel to have so many to provide for at once.

February 15th. Meerut.
We leave this place tomorrow and three marches will take us to Delhi. I have a grand idea of Delhi. I think I had a grand idea of it when I was in Europe. I wonder whether I had. Do you happen to think grandly of Delhi? The King is a great man who would not see the Governor-General unless he sits upon the smaller chair. The Governor-General, who is also a great man, will not do any such thing, so they will not meet . . .

We are beginning to get into civilised ways and go out to ride on the course so it is time to move.

February 17th. Delhi.
This is quite as grand, dear, as I meant it to be. As we rode over the bridge, the first view of the city was the finest and most solid sight of

131

eastern magnificence that we have seen. Such gateways, and the enormous Palace with its two miles of walls and battlements round it, and old mosques without end rising from among the other buildings. The streets too look busy, and though the King is no longer the rich King he used to be, the city looks as if pains were taken to keep up the buildings worth preserving.

We went to the Jammu Masjid this afternoon – an enormous Mosque built of granite and marble. I do not think I have ever seen a building which gave me such an idea of what man can do or any building so impossible to attempt to describe. The courts are inlaid with marble, the domes are of solid marble and the building seems to cover the space of a small town. The walls round the palace are sixty feet high and entirely built of large blocks of red granite. We have not been to see the Palace yet. I mean tomorrow to go and sketch a part of the old city, which is now nothing but ruins, the only curious thing left standing is a pillar forty feet high made of one stone.

February 18th. Delhi.

. . . We have been to see the palace today where there are melancholy remains of former magnificence. Long white marble halls inlaid with precious stones, most of which have been picked out and sold, and nothing put in their places. Beautiful agate fountains where the lowest servants seem to sleep and cook if they like. The King was sitting in the gardens with a single servant behind him keeping off the flies. No-one approaches him without great ceremony. Many of his relations will live and die without passing the walls of that palace – his female ones, of course, but many of the others, too.

In the hall of audience where the pavement and pillars are still inlaid with precious stones, there is the Arabic original of Moore's line: 'If there's bliss upon earth, it is this, it is this.'

February 21st. Delhi.

We are encamped ten miles from Delhi today for the sake of seeing the Kootub [Minar] and the ruins round it. And I do not think I have yet seen anything so beautiful – the beauty, though, of extreme desolation. We stopped on our way to see the tombs of their Kings. It is worth dying here to have a great temple built and called a tomb. Here there were gardens and fountains, and a very large marble temple, and in a small marble one was the real tomb, covered with gold tissue and the King's sword and shield upon it. One man always remains with a peacock chourie to keep off the flies, and two men are always reading the Koran to him. They are always there, day and night, and that is the case at most of the royal tombs here.

On the other side is one of the ruined gateways which lead to the Kootub, and this is the pillar itself [see p. 134]. I had a sort of fancy, dear, that a pillar could not be imposing looking, that all pillars would more or less resemble the Monument, but this of red granite, with its magnificent carving and a whole city of ruins at its feet, is a sight that must strike anybody. It is 290 feet high and 150 feet in circumference. It is fluted with round and triangular flutings, which I have not expressed there, but I have sketched on the other side. Nobody knows when it was built. There are Hindoo temples round it and they claim it, and say that the Mahommedans tried to build another like it and turn it into the minaret of a mosque and failed.

Before we settled to sketch this morning we went to one of those great wells like the one I sent you a sketch of. There are a set of men there called jumpers, who jump from the wall above and splash into the water below, a distance between sixty and seventy feet. It is the thing that has given me the greatest thrill I ever felt. They do not turn over in the air but go down quite perpendicularly, the soles of their feet first go into the water. As one followed the other and ran up the steps of the well and stood dripping on the edge ready to jump again, though I expected to see them dashed to pieces, by a sort of fascination I could not help looking at them. The hyenas were crying round the tomb last night, and one came into our French servant's tent. I thought of Gazelle with complacency. A faquir jumped from the top of this pillar the other day, as an exemplary way of ending his life.

February 22nd. Delhi.
I do not think that the European part of the community at Delhi is distinguished in any way, except perhaps that the female part of it are addicted to black mittens of their own making, with large brassy looking bracelets over them.

How odd of me not to have told you that the very first person I saw at the very first ball at Meerut was Mrs Parkes. How she got there nobody knows and nobody will ever know. The day after we got here they got up a morning review for us – blew up mines and took a fort, and not only a fort but Mrs Parkes, for as the smoke blew off she was discovered riding. If she were not so fat I should say she was something supernatural. My spirit is broke about her. I dare say we shall find her settled in our home at Simla and shall not have strength to turn her out.

I hope when it arrives you will like this bracelet I have made you buy yourself. I have seen some of the same kind here – not half so handsome and six times the price. I begin to think I must have done well for you.

February 23rd. Delhi.
You see this is another of those wells which people jump into, and those black things are meant not for frogs but men [see p. 137]. These jumpers were much more appalling to see than the others. They started at the top of that high dome and along all the roofs, and after giving one leap forwards to clear all the impediments in their way, come down in the perpendicular position I have put them in. If you could see the height of the buildings they jump from you would wonder they are not dashed to pieces or caught upon the roofs between them and the water. The great sight near here is Humayun's tomb, a great red and white marble building which I did not attempt, but there is a smaller tomb on the other side, and every separate tomb that it contains is of carved white marble, often carving like lace – perfectly beautiful.

If ever you have been driven to read a modern Indian book, I daresay you have read about Colonel Skinner – a native Colonel, very black, much better society than any of the white Colonels we meet here, and who has done many warlike wonders. He is staying here and is a very fine old man. We went on Sunday to a large church he has built, and there is a mosque he has also built very near it. He told me that where is God, there is religion, but I suppose he calls himself a Mussulman. There are any number of beautiful Mrs Skinners, and when he asked us if we would like to have native curiosities sent us to look at – he said they would be things only to look at, not to buy, 'for I must borrow them from all my mothers and all my grandmothers, very particular old women.' His brother was not so happy in domestic life, and one day in a fit of distrust, actually cut all his wives' throats and then destroyed himself.

Colonel Skinner commands a troop called Skinner's Horse in strange, wild-looking dresses. We went last night to a nautch at his house – very well worth seeing. One of the old Hindu plays were acted – only high-caste Brahmins can act that – boys dressed up to represent their Gods and Goddesses. Krishna was a beautiful figure. In fact their acting is little more than representing a succession of tableaux and singing a noisy sort of recitative between. The nautch girls' dresses as usual were splendid and their dancing very graceful, but there is a great sameness in it, and though some people admire their singing, to me it sounds positively frightful. One of them though sang a song to prove that

George's countenance was so resplendent, it was impossible to look at it.
I have turned my eyes the other way ever since.

February 25th
We are two marches from Delhi on the road to Kurnaul and had a most
disastrous night of it last night. This is a very bad part of the country and
there were supposed to be swarms of thieves about the camp, not a very
uncommon occurrence. At three in the morning one of Mr Macnaghten's
servants seized a man who was running off with something. As is almost
invariably the case the man instantly stabbed him to the heart and he died
on the spot. I heard the shrieks of the other servants, but fancied it was
only a common thieving occurrence. They have taken the man who was
supposed to have done it, but in the confusion that ensued it was very
difficult to identify him. Some of the other servants with the advanced
camp were wounded and beaten, and almost all the people in both camps
have had something stolen from them. The first thing we saw from the
road this morning was Mrs Macnaghten wandering madly over the
country on an elephant looking for a box of papers that had been taken
and they have been found – the thieves were evidently bored with them.
Tonight the exemplary irregular horse people will patrol the road and I
place the most implicit confidence in *them*.

February 27th. Paneeput.
This is the remains of a great city and a great battle was fought near the
ground where we are encamped – it was the last great struggle Maha-
rattas made against the Mahommedans – you remember all about that
of course. I don't but I know that Panee is Hindoostani for water so put
is probably Hindoostani for loo, and this is the real field of Waterloo. In
the mean time, the struggle being over, William and I went out this
afternoon, he after partridges and I after sketches, and he found no
birds and I only found that well. There has been no rain yet and even in
this part of the country they water all the crops that do grow and that is
the sort of refined well they have. The bullocks turn the handle which
turns the wheel which turns the other wheel covered with Kedgeree pots
and they fish up water and empty themselves into that trunk of a tree
hollowed as a trough and that empties itself into drains which run along
their fields and it all does very well, but it is the sort of thing that makes
the refined spirits of the camp shrug up their shoulders and say 'Poo-er
Cree-churs', that sort of prolonged poor creature which at once shows
their immeasurable inferiority [see p. 138].

137

There are shocking accounts from the neighbourhood of Cawnpore where we saw so much distress. There has been no rain, all the cattle have long died and men did the work of bullocks to draw water for some of their fields, but even in these the crops have failed and the people are dying by hundreds and those who can are wandering to other parts. There is no visible distress here but the country is dreadfully burnt up and promises ill for next year.

March 1st
We shall arrive at Kurnaul tomorrow. Again last night the officer on guard who goes on into the advanced camp had his tent stripped of everything while he and his servants were asleep in it and round it. They

let down one side of his tent and carried off even his camel trunks. The magistrates take all this robbing as a personal insult to themselves and say in a sort of piqued tone 'Do you not think your own people do it?' – when this is notoriously the most robbing district in India. The consequence is that most of the things go on much earlier than they used to do. That is the figure Captain Cunningham presents on the opposite side. All the secretaries are allowed two long tents, but the aide-de-camps only one long tent and one sleeping tent – the thing you see which just holds a bed. For some reason they have taken to sending on their long tents early in the afternoon – you see it and the rest of his property going off per favour of elephant, camel, and cart. The trunks he necessarily keeps are outside the tent that the sentinel may keep an eye on them and there he sits, a touching picture.

I am very low about getting no more letters – no ships, no overland dispatch, no nothing. They have brought round all the little ponies we are to ride in the hills – shocking looking little animals – bad editions of

139

shetland ponies with mouths that no human tugging can make an impression upon. What figures we shall all be ambling along upon them. Rolla has got the most lovely new dress – crimson velvet bound with real gold, long sleeves which suit his black hands particularly – it was made by the best tailor in the camp and fits him to perfection.

March 3rd. Kurnaul.

If anybody had told me this was Cawnpore again I should have been puzzled how to give them a decided contradiction. There is a long flat dusty plain and a church and a cantonment and a few bonnets of no particular shape driving up and down a road of no particular determination and a few young bored-looking officers riding one way and a great many old bored-looking officers riding another. But they have one advantage, they point to a remarkably cloudless sky and an horizon which has nothing to bound it and say, 'If this happened to be a clear day and you would look that way, well and steadily, you would be able to see the outline of the hills – we pique ourselves on our view of the hills – that is the direction – you perceive something – a sort of thickness – as far as the eye can reach.' And then, after a pause that the eye may have had time to reach, they add in a tone of compassion, 'You are a little short-sighted, perhaps?'

That very masterly portrait is of a man who came to see us today – a very remarkable man. When William was in this country before, he knew him well as a high-caste brahmin. Now he is one of the few natives who profess a frank Christianity. Some time ago he was ordained. He has set up a school and is making converts. I forget the name of the missionary who converted him, but he says Mrs Sherwood* and her stories did more for him than anybody else. Mrs Wimberley was talking to him while I was sketching him and he seemed to have a perfect knowledge of the Bible. He said there was more hope of making converts among the Hindoos than the Mussulmen for 'it seems to me that mussulmen have stolen bits of our Bible to make up theirs and they will not give up their stolen goods.' When he laughs he is like a black Sydney Smith.[†]

March 4th

Two years ago today since we landed in this country, at least, so they say

* A pious evangelical author of many very popular tracts and books, who spent part of her life in India. *The Indian Pilgrim* and *Little Henry and His Bearer* were both translated into Hindustani.
† Canon of St Paul's and the wittiest man of his day.

here. I very much suspect you have been living twenty in England. I think I trace it in the papers 'a new reign – new cabriolets – war with Canada – dependence on the Queen's army'. When we were in England nobody ever used such words and we are so very slow here it is clear that we reckon our years slowly. And then our faculties are really wearing very fast. I thought I was growing cleverer but I am not. I passed five minutes last night proving to George how very provoking it was that our camp clocks should always be too slow, striking ten minutes before any other clocks, and upon his innocently remarking 'Too fast, you mean', I answered tartly – 'No, too slow. I said before, not after'. I believe that is a fair instance of the average calibre of our intellect and depth of power of reasoning.

We have done a very great ball and a very great dinner. I never before saw so many large joints of so many large beasts upon one table. I am certain they served up a baked shoulder of elephant and called it a shoulder of mutton. Then, as always happens to me at these great dinners, I lost my head as to the stage of dinner we had arrived at and in the middle of the second course asked my neighbour to give me some wine, thinking we were at the end of dessert and desperate at having none offered to me. We ate on for a whole hour after that.

That is a little native boy with white mice for sale. If he had been in England he would have been an Italian boy. When I tried to sketch him he carefully shut his eyes and probably flattered himself that he was not to be seen.

March 6th. Kurnaul.
We were to have left Kurnaul today but the servants petitioned to stay, for this is one of their great festivals. I remember writing to you about it last year from Rajmahal when all the mussulman servants were sacrificing their little kids. Today, being near no particularly sacred place, they prepared two tents, one for a place of worship, the other for a place of sacrifice. The Nazir, George's chief servant, who is a very great man among them, provided a camel, most of the others sheep which are easier to be procured here than kids. They are at this moment, two or three hundred of them, kneeling in an open tent opposite with their heads lowered down to the ground – all of them dressed in white and their priest standing in the middle of them reading out of some manuscript book. The other tent, where the animals are assembled for sacrifice, is happily a little further off.

William has set off today to meet General Churchill and Colonel Arnold who commands his old regiment the 16th Lancers, and they are going for three weeks into the deep jungle where tigers abound and will meet us others at Simla or the foot of the hills. This country is just as bad about its interior as its exterior posts – if all the tigers in the world take to eat William up he will find no means of sending me a letter to tell me of it.

I was interrupted by the Nazir walking in with as many servants as my tent will hold and they stood with their hands clasped while he said how they had been praying to their gods for us all, and how they were going to offer sacrifice for us as well as themselves. They are always very graceful and correct about any speech they have to make, and would make everybody believe that their first object on earth is our healths and prosperities, whereas I believe they look upon us as a singularly depraved set of heathens.

There are times when a sickening feeling comes over me at being in 'a heathen land' – at Delhi when towards sunset voices from the great mosque were calling the people to prayer, and sometimes in small temples where there is the noisy worship of some grinning idol – and still from time to time horrible facts come out about human sacrifices. I suppose at this moment when the rage for education is very great and the mussulman chiefs no longer oppose it, there is more hope of converts being made, but considering the time Europeans have been in the country it seems quite extraordinary that with a *very* few individual exceptions not one native seems to have adopted a single European custom. Somebody once imported on speculation a thousand Scotch ploughs, all of which were left upon his hands. The natives walk contentedly about with little apologies for ploughs on their shoulders in the shape of two sticks with a blade stuck in them.

143

March 8th

We have had heaps of overland letters but none from you, dear, this time. No ships ever come, not even your own particular ship, and I want another letter from you . . .

I got a letter from William today. He had just got out of his palan-quin and found his camp surrounded by monkeys, his horses frightened out of their wits by them, two of his servants in fevers and he with only a turn-screw to bleed them with. He was within three days' march of the tiger jungle and his companions. He had got twelve of the Rajah of Oude's elephants with him, and the Rajah of Rampore, the owner of the elephant carriage, and thirty more elephants were to join them. That Rajah is a great sporting character, but is a little apt to go out not par-ticularly sober, so it is to be hoped that they will only load his gun with powder.

There has been a great deal of rain here and there are green crops and green trees, and the hills in the distance. Now I see it again in any shape but my own dusty gown, green is certainly a very pretty colour. There is nothing to sketch and I tried those tiresome camels again in mere absence of mind this afternoon. We get to Saharanpur tomorrow, when the camp breaks up almost entirely. We even part Rosenkrantz and Guildenstern; one will go with us and the other find his own way to the hills.

March 11th. Saharanpur.

I did that man just now – surreptitiously while we were receiving visits. Mr Torrens says he is a Gooja and I cleverly asked whether he came from America and poked people's eyes out with his thumb, but it appears they are a set of this country's people who have a particular fancy for stealing buffaloes – otherwise are exemplary characters and well off, living on the fat of the land. I think there's a shade of genius in that sketch, don't you? By the time I am turned eighty and cannot see, I expect to be clever about drawing figures.

This is a treasure of a little station – only two ladies in it – one of them a Miss Bacon who is living with her brother, is handsome and has a great deal to say. There is a botanical garden too – with a great many drives about it and fruit that Rolla likes. The view of the many mountains too is good and decided, and the air from them quite cool. When I get fairly to the foot of the hills, which I shall in four or five days, I shall send this journal off to you – for I shall be driven to my large sketch book.

This is the hooghly festival,* and all the hindu servants just came in

* the Hindu Spring festival of Holi

144

145

smeared over with pink and blue powder and an offering of sweetmeats which I touched, and offered them rupees which they did more than touch. They will be all drunk tonight which always happens at this festival and seldom at any other time.

March 13th

We have got such a satisfactory little encampment today. We left the large camp at Saharanpur, and have nobody with us but the Torrens, Macnaghtens, MacGregor, Macintosh and Byrne. Our tents are in a grove of trees – and a slight sprinkling of camels and elephants and people cooking – and Rolla in his red dress jumping from one mangoe tree to another with flights of parroquets round him – and in the distance, dear, such a magnificent line of hills with snowy mountains behind them – one of them is the highest mountain in the world they say – and I believe them and of course feel it doubly pleasant to look at it.

This break-up of the camp seems to agree with the happiness of people in general: Mrs Macnaghten is happy because she is following the Governor-General's division which she feels due to her rank – Mr Torrens is happy because he can go every day after a tiger which he is quite certain not to find – General Casement is happy because he is in command of the Hawkins and the other camp and now, as he told us, can march at whatever hour the ladies like best, poor Mrs Wimberley (the only other lady) never being allowed a choice on the subject. We are all dreadfully jealous about the shawls and bracelets he gave Mrs Hawkins at Delhi. Mrs Colvin is happy because the day after we left Kurnaul she became the mother of a boy and has got Colvin back again – Mrs Codrington is happy because she is expecting to become the mother of a boy at Meerut, and has got Codrington back again, and Mrs Thomasson is happy because she has run up dak to Simla to become the mother of a boy and Thomasson is running up after her. William is I hope happy, with a tiger on one side of him and a wild elephant on the other. The aide-de-camps are all happy because there are no levees or durbars, and we are happy because the country is pretty, the climate good and few of our civilized fellow-creatures within reach.

That is one of Colonel Skinner's men, but I had no room for his boots and the thinness of the paper checks the grandeur of my ideas about colouring. These people on their horses look wild and well – some of them are following our camp, so are the irregular horse-people, in case, I suppose, that we should want to go to war with a neighbouring tribe.

March 14th

We moved on only eight miles today, because George is gone off after a tiger. They all went out after one yesterday, fell in with plenty of deer, and by their own confession shot excessively ill. In fact the deer at last fairly drew up and looked at them and their elephants to see what they were made of; however they went through beautiful country. George declared the sun was not hot, Mr Macnaghten in a very large pair of blue spectacles took aim at everything and killed nothing particular.

We were in a beautiful encampment, hills and mountains all about us; we are in a still more beautiful one in the Dhera pass, where the road seems to be enclosed by hills.

March 15th. Dhera Dhun.

That is my old tailor and very like him. Where he puts his legs and feet when he works, nobody has ever been able to discover. A lady asked me the other day whether I allowed my tailor thread to work with, and upon my laughing and asking what else he could work with, she said, it was an extravagance all ladies did not give in to – she made her tailor untwist the cloth he was to hem, and twist his own thread, but 'poor creet-churs, in a house like yours they all get lifted up'. A great many ladies always have their tailors to work in their drawing-rooms – and their chief occupation seems to be to watch them.

They shot worse than they did the day before, and all confess it except dear Byrne, who said complacently, 'I shot remarkably well' – and when I asked him what he had killed, he said, 'I shot a snipe and saw a bear', and he *was* perfectly convinced he shot remarkably well, because he killed that snipe. In fact it is too early in the year to find tigers here – bears do clamber about the hills they say, and there are deer and peacocks and monkeys in the jungles – but in this part of the world they set about shooting later in the day than I can bear to be out and as to Emily, she would not stir out of the tent at all if there were certain tidings of a tiger.

March 16th. Dhera.

His Excellency all of a sudden yesterday, when we thought we were turned in for the day, suggested that we should march on here, it being only five miles off and a station at the foot of the hills. It was an odd eastern despot kind of idea, for we never had marched after dinner before, and dear Byrne thought over his camels and elephants and looked calmly astounded. However all our little goods were instantly

sent off – our beds were I may say taken from under us – and after dinner we followed them by torch light.

I really do think that the 'men in authority' here lead very enviable lives, and they are the first Indian men of authority about whom such a thought has crossed my mind. Nothing can be more beautiful than the country with its line of mountains. For seven months in the year the climate seems to be perfect too and when the hot winds set in, a ten miles' drive will take them up the hills to a real cold bracing climate. Today in the tents it is hot from the sun beating on them; tomorrow we shall be at Colonel Young's house at Mussorie in fur shoes and cloaks – the thermometers in the rooms where fires are burning, at 55. Our tents are filled with English flowers of every description they have sent us from their gardens – they have farms which flourish – and Colonel Young, who is the chief man here, commands a most interesting native regiment, the Gourkas. I should say they will fight less well now we have brought them down to our English drilling and nonsense, but there was a time, when four or five hundred of them in their hills beat our troops considerably and kept beating them for a whole year. They are the most dwarfish race that I ever saw and look like a little set of children in their dark uniforms. Last year a party of them fell in with a tiger on the road we travelled yesterday. They were on foot and had no guns, but they made a circle round him, and when he charged one side they cut at him on the other with their swords, and so killed him. There was a little Gourka following the regiment in an odd looking uniform with flowers stuck in his helmet instead of a feather and a very large sword with which he saluted George – he is an idiot and acts as fool to the regiment and is allowed to follow it at all times . . .

March 17th. Mussorie.
. . . Now we are at Mussorie, seven thousand feet higher than we were yesterday. How it ever entered human creatures' heads to settle here I cannot imagine, but having done it nothing can be more beautiful – hills above and hills below and the snowy mountains within reach. There seems to be literally not an inch of level ground. The foundations of most of the houses are poles stuck in the side of a hill. People's houses which look within a quarter-of-a-mile turn out to be three or four miles off because of the deep ravines between. Of course no carriage can come here, but we were carried part of the way in jonpauns, sort of open sedan chairs. After three miles of them I took courage and got on my pony, and it was a valuable little animal and climbed up the side of the hills like a cat. I have a rule not to be frightened at anything but it is

rather frightful at first, climbing up the perpendicular paths with not a rail to keep oneself and pony from rolling down some thousand feet of precipice at the side. Every now and then somebody said in a cheerful tone, 'It's astonishing how seldom accidents *do* happen. This is the hill where poor Major Burton and his pony rolled down and were killed on the spot, but then a snake crossed the path and that always frightens a pony.' So I kept looking out for snakes.

It is not the least too cold – quite perfect, with fires burning in containers, and carpeted houses. We are staying at Col. Young's and are very comfortable, in a regular cottage. Mrs Young is still in the plains. There is a large hotel just built on a hill here, and slate billiard tables in it. It is impossible in this book to attempt a sketch of the mountains, but if you were to see where we are and upon what we are looking down, you would wonder how hotels and slate billiard tables get here. All the materials for building are brought from the plains.

The rhododendron trees are splendid – long timber trees, one mass of the deepest crimson blossoms. Our Bengalee servants are frightened out of their senses. They all walk about with long sticks to save themselves in case they should slip over the edge of the precipice this house is built upon. They suffer too with the cold. We are able to be out any hour of the day and to be sure there is pleasure in thinking we have seven months of these mountains and then four months march before we get back to Calcutta. There is a want of water in these mountains, but it is impossible to imagine grander or more awful looking scenery. As a little child said the other day, looking at the snowy range which towers above all the others: 'We seem to have got upon the steps which are leading up to heaven.'

I shall not write you any more journal now till we are upon the road down again, but I shall write you a great many letters which you will probably never receive. I believe you will receive this in tatters. This book was bought at Calcutta and the paper is literally brittle with the heat. I foresee that by the time I have been three or four weeks in this climate and among such scenery I shall rescind all I have ever said about India, and declare it is the only place to live in.

Captain MacGregor just came in looking pale and breathless, and said, 'I have just seen Mrs Parkes – *here!* She has sent her remembrance to Lord Auckland and the Miss Edens, and is delighted to think she has fallen in with them again, and hopes soon to make her way to Simla.' There is something very horrid and unearthly in all this – nobody ever had a fat attendant spirit before.

There are bad stories of leopards rushing into houses and carrying off little dogs from under the eyes of their mistresses. Great exertions are

151

making to establish a regular supply of fruit from the plains for Rolla. I am beginning to think well of the civil service – it stirs so much activity upon this particular point. Captain Champneys sent word that Gazelle's spirits were not good, which disturbs me. Chance flourishes and must wear a suit of armour to defend himself against the leopards. The air of Delhi proved too much for the Honourable John. He grew ill there and though I had him fully fed the day before we marched, he did not follow, and the next day they told me he was dying of old age. There was something very shocking in having left him as food for the jackals. I felt like Goneril and Regan both. The only thing that distresses me on the march is the quantity of animal suffering that is to be seen. The very poorest camp followers have little ponies which they load

152

beyond all belief and feed on next to nothing, and then urge them on till they drop down dead. Now and then the elephant mahouts are savage beyond description, but they are always turned away if it is found out.

March 18th

We go down to the plains again this afternoon as the march across the hills is too difficult, and today I will really finish this and send it to somebody at Calcutta to forward to England. When I came to look over my sketches I am rather ashamed of them, but then you know I never pretended to draw and this is only for you and Emma and Lord Robert if they like, and you need not say how bad they are. It is a good time since we were at Rajmahal and I have not yet heard from you of the arrival of that book – so tiresome.

We took a ride yesterday which made me giddy, such a depth of precipice within a few inches of us and the ponies seeming to hang back from the perpendicular paths they had to go down. Of course, when I asked at one place where I felt particularly dizzy why that stone was stuck by the path, it turned out a soldier had been dashed to pieces there, and the miraculous escapes of individuals whose ponies had been dashed to pieces while they had been caught in the roots of trees seem to be without end. In a day or two, though, the beauty of the scenery would make one forget the danger, and at Simla the roads are wider and better than they are here. That is a jonpaun and those little bearers go at a wonderful pace with them, two in the shafts, two at the end of the pole which passes between the shafts . . . We found just now George's little French servant Mars with that misfortunate creature Ariffe, whom he was conducting up one of the highest precipices – Mars in shrieks of laughter, and Ariffe not white but yellow with terror, a large stick in his hand. Twice he had thrown himself down flat and declared he would go no further, but Mars had rallied him into trying again.

I have got a letter from William which has been a week coming and he was just setting off with certain intelligence of a tiger, the first they had heard of.

I do not much like finishing like this, it feels like taking leave of you again. I shall write overland in a fortnight and this will come long after that letter, I dare say.

God bless you, dearest,
Your most affectionate
F.H.E.

Third Journal

To the Court
of Ranjit Singh

The party reached Simla in the Himalayan foothills on April 3rd 1838 and stayed there to avoid the hot season in the plains, until the Autumn. Emily wrote to a friend in England as soon as they arrived: 'Well, it really is worth all the trouble. Such a beautiful place, and our house only wanting the good furniture and carpets we have brought to be perfect. Views only too lovely; deep valleys on the drawing-room side on the west, and the snowy range on the dining-room side . . . and the climate! No wonder I could not live down below! We never were allowed a scrap of air to breathe. Now I come back to the air again I remember all about it. It is a cool sort of stuff, refreshing, sweet, and apparently pleasant to the lungs. We have fires in every room and the windows open; red rhododendron trees bloom in every direction, and beautiful walks like English shrubberies cut on all sides of the hills. Good! I see this to be the best part of India.'

They settled down, and for the first time since they had come to India, the long sense of strain lightened a little. Fanny noticed the ceilings without punkahs, and people riding and walking in the sunshine; it made her feel like the same species of human being she had been in England.

Mr Macnaghten was going to Lahore. Now that the decision to depose Dost Mohammed and put Shah Shuja on the throne of Afghanistan had been taken, the Governor-General's Political Secretary was to discuss the proposed new treaty with Ranjit Singh as soon as possible. But everything had to be done with due form. At the end of April, 1838, a deputation of Sikh chiefs and envoys arrived from Ranjit Singh to wait on the Governor-General, bringing messages and gifts. Soon after their arrival, George held a durbar for them. Major Byrne usually managed to make the durbar tent look like a drying ground at a laundress's by covering the ground with white cloth. There would be a change at *this* durbar. Emily and Fanny took charge of the arrangements themselves, and paid no attention to Byrne. They threw open the folding doors between the principal rooms, and covered the floor with scarlet linen.

George sat on a gilt chair and listened for an hour to Major Byrne translating flowery nonsense. George hoped that the deputation had not
suffered from the rains, which had come on heavily since their arrival.
They replied that the canopy of friendship had interposed such a thick
cloud that their tents had remained quite dry. Which was touching, as
Emily knew that their tents had been so soaked through, they had been
obliged to hire the only empty house in Simla. They then conveyed the
Maharajah's message, which was to say that the roses had bloomed in the
garden of friendship and the nightingales had sung in the bowers of affection sweeter than ever, since the two Powers had approached each other.

The real negotiations, the firm details of their joint policy with regard
to Afghanistan, were for Macnaghten to arrange when he met Ranjit
Singh in May. Ranjit was more than a match for the British party when it
came to negotiation and although he eventually signed an agreement, it
was not on the lines originally envisaged. There was no question any
longer of the Sikhs taking on Dost Mohammed by themselves. It was to
be a joint Anglo-Sikh expedition.

Fanny and Emily continued to scandalise Simla society: holding a
dance for the Sikh envoys to which English ladies were also expected to
come; giving full support to amateur theatricals put on by the half-caste
Anglo-Indian community. As Emily said, with her usual irony, 'We, with
our pure Norman or Saxon blood, cannot really think contemptuously
enough of them . . .' Again, when the Simla ladies objected to the idea
of this community contributing to a charitable sale of work, Emily
pointed out tartly that the black would not come off on their fancy-work.

Although the Persian siege of Herat ended in September, the plan for
proceeding against Dost Mohammed went ahead, and the Governor-
General's party resumed its progress towards the meeting with Ranjit
Singh in November 1838.

November 9th 1838. Buddee.
I am deeply distressed about the shape of this book, long and bad, but I
was very lucky to get this on the top of the Himalayas – real Chinese
paper.* All the English drawing paper turns into something like a greasy
sponge. Whether you will be most bored reading my writing after the
fashion of 'Elegant extracts' in two columns, or meandering interminably
along the page, I do not know – but I rather like the column plot the best.
I sent you a long overland letter this very day, so you know how we got
down the hills and arrived here; this writing effort is only to break myself
in for a journal again.

* Fanny was starting this journal in a new book.

There is a mud fort of some merit just above us, but I am not enough rested from our descent even to look at it. Our tents look as if we had never left them – chairs, sofas, tables, have all fallen naturally into their own niches – so has George, and a miserable niche he thinks it. As usual I am very comfortable. We have left winter to come to summer, but a very moderate kind of summer, for the cold season is just beginning.

As I told you, we have no ladies with us but Mrs Macnaghten for a little till Mr Macnaghten goes to travel about with the Shah Soojah and his army, and then *she* returns to the hills, for Captain Burnes, the Bokhara man, whom you have gone and made Sir Alexander, declares that no woman can shew herself in that part of the world.* All the other husbands have taken advantage of Sir H. Fane's† orders to *his* army to leave behind 'all women and other superfluous baggage' – why that order was to influence our camp nobody but the husbands discovered . . .

I believe that we are on the borders of Cachemire which Moore wrote about; there are sugar canes but no roses – sugar canes would probably spoil the metre‡. . .

November 10th. Nalleeghur.
We staid all yesterday at Buddee to let the things come up – and what is wonderful they really have come up – all except Mr Macnaghten's plate chest; great terror reigns in the camp on account of that – what will Shah Soojah who eats with his fingers think of Macnaghten if he does the same thing?

We came through a pretty bit of country today – still a little hilly – and streams running with fish in them; it is seldom streams run in India, and seldomer that there is fish fit to eat. There were flights of parroquets too. The Commissariat have taken our smooth elephants, and I tried one this morning which moved as a great mountain would move if it were playful – very nearly dislocated my limbs.

November 11th. Nalleeghur.
We are [still] here because it is Sunday. That is a fragment of the Rajah of Nalleeghur's house; he has a beautiful little kingdom on the hills and a palace of great beauty too, but just as I began to sketch it a thunder

* Sir Alexander Burnes, British Intelligence officer, author of *Travels Into Bokhara*, 1834.
† See entry for November 27th.
‡ A reference to Thomas Moore's poem *Lalla Rookh*.

storm came on, so that is the wretched result and I could only put in one stone peacock. He was there himself, a melancholy old man, grieving for the loss of his best Mrs Nalleeghur – the only one he really liked and she died lately. The rain and thunder are awful, and I expect the tents will be down on our heads before morning.

November 12th. Roopur.
Such a day, dear – it is pouring, and you do not know what it is to have a pouring day in tents: the roof wet above and the floor wet below, the servants wet and miserable, the camels slipping and falling with their loads, the carts sticking in the mud with theirs, the beds a little wet, the sofa wetter still, the armchairs wettest of all. Then on the rain goes on, and the ground grows softer and the thunder sounds louder and the wind blows harder, with the pleasing uncertainty whether every gust will not bring the dripping canvas down upon the ground with no intervening obstacle but oneself. The tents we have left at the last ground will probably be so heavy with wet, the elephants will not be able to carry them to the next ground, and we shall be kept here in this damp misery. George in his detestation of a camp is almost happy with this concentration of horrors.

There is a report which disturbs my peace of mind, that Myra my best ayah, and her husband and two of William's grooms, were *thugged* on their way to Calcutta. The magistrate who told me of it said he partly believed it. We have written to the first station through which they ought to have passed for tidings of them. They had high wages and bought many shawls and trinkets, and were well aware that their journey was a dangerous proceeding. It grows wetter and colder and I have sent Rolla to the french cook that he may put him by the fire – I hope he will not skin and roast him.

November 13th
We did move at last today and our encampment is what may be called a shame to be seen – a large coat of mud over all our tents because they were moved wet – a tidy set of gipsies would be ashamed of us. We are in the Sikh country now . . . which has heaps of little forts about . . . The Sikhs are so turbulent among themselves they like to have their own little fortifications. Four Sikh ladies near here, who live in separate towers in one fort, show the little piques they take with each other by firing great guns across – sometimes their wars run to length.

The roads were dreadful today – bullocks died on the march, and Paul, my beautiful old arab, is declared not to be up to them, and as he

160

never minds how much firing and row there is round him, it goes to my heart to give him up. Selim, the horse I am to ride, Serjeant Web the man at the head of the stables, calls 'a fine fiery little orse that nothing tries – he kicks a little sometimes but nothing to sinify'. Pleasant!

November 14th. Musheewara.
Mind that you pronounce well the names of all the towns I write – it would mortify me exceedingly if you did not.

The roads were worse than ever this morning, but the fiery little orse carried me very well. There was a remarkably fine white bullock dead by its cart, and everybody who passed asked in a tone of commiseration whose bullock it was. When they found it was only the Company's they said Oh – and did not mind – as if the bullock had suffered a bit less. Rolla has found a wheel carriage quite insufferable, it keeps him so long from his breakfast, so now he travels in my palanquin.

This is a lawless country and the servants are all frightened, and by way of making them better our ayahs were stopped last night by a man with a drawn sword – who found nothing to take but my ayah's cooking things. My new ayah, Mary O'Neil, is a very attractive person, a half caste; she was brought up at the Military orphan school – was married at twelve years old to a man forty years older than herself who came and *chose* her from the school as was then the custom – she is little more than twenty now. He went home to England leaving her here. She had six sisters who all married in the same way, most of them happily. She is very highly spoken of herself and takes my fancy.

That man came when we were sitting before the tents this afternoon. The monkey who is riding upon the stick had a decided genius for dancing. The goat had no decided genius for anything but standing so [see p. 162].

November 15th
We encamp now every day on sandy plains so the face of the country may be called uniform rather than picturesque . . . Have not I got your No 31? Such a treasure of a letter just after all the foreigners were about London, and you had got my first journal and the tortoise shell fan and liked them both, so lucky. I am still owed No 30 and 29.

November 16th. Loodiana.
We are to halt here for two days and it is quite time for a rest. The roads break not only the bullocks' and camels' hearts but ours. I shewed

wonderful courage this morning – put myself upon Selim with the trying certainty that there would be forty horses galloping round us and
the howitzers banging in our faces before we should reach the city.
Those howitzers are some of the presents to be given Runjeet and have
been made on purpose very much ornamented – but just as effective as
if they had no ornament at all. They shattered me very much but Selim
stood them well.

There is no great beauty about the city though it looks clean – but
such of the Cashmirian women as do appear are handsome. The inhabitants are a curious mixture of Persians, Cashmirians, and Sikhs. The
account of robberies which greeted us upon our arrival at the advanced
camp was awful. Two of the sepoys had been stabbed by some robbers
and were dead. I found my ayah with her teeth actually chattering from
fright. 'Not but what Sergeant . . . was very good for he came round and

woke us and told us to sleep light, for two men had been murdered.'
Such a clever way to ensure a pleasant night.

We have been receiving the Loodiana world, which consists in one
female. All the rest have gone away, because they declared that without
their husbands in this country they cannot defend themselves against
robbers. I was excessively taken by the one who did come. She was an
enormous dark woman who ended many of her sentences by saying,
'Oh, think of us poor unprotected females'. And then she talked of one
lady who had been 'the reigning belle of the station', and when I asked
where she was now, she said 'Mrs G. has made a step in life. She is
removed to the Thuggie department'. I hope she will not remain in the
Thuggie department.

November 17th. Loodiana.
We had an enormous dinner at Major Wade's* yesterday, and the city
was illuminated after the native way in long lines of little lamps.
Nothing could be prettier. They had laid out, in long lines upon a green
in front of the house, a whole garden of light, with little flames as thick
as could be forming all sorts of paths and walks, and turbaned people
going about like gardeners with watering pots, throwing oil to keep up
the lights. Put turbans on all the servants next time you have lights in
the garden at Westminster House. I cannot recollect whether you call it
Westminster House or Grosvenor House. There used to be a square of
the same name – that I'm sure of.

November 18th, Sunday. Loodiana.
I shall always put when it is Sunday, that we may be sure we are living in
the same year. Not like the old general who sate between me and
William at dinner yesterday. He refused to answer any question asked
him, and baffled me utterly. But he did ask William a question and I
heard it. He said suddenly: 'Pray can you tell me, are we in the year
1838 or 1839?' and William, hoping he had to sign an important paper
next morning, answered: '1839'.

I sketched those turbans yesterday while George was holding a
durbar. They were straying about outside. Soojah's son came to it and,
having no elephant as well as no kingdom, they sent my own particular
one to fetch him. I was very much overcome when I saw him arrive upon
that. I am not at all sure that I like to be made to take so decided a part
in a war against Dost Mohamed. The servants dressed up Rolla and

* Claude Wade, British agent to the Sikh kingdom at Ludhiana.

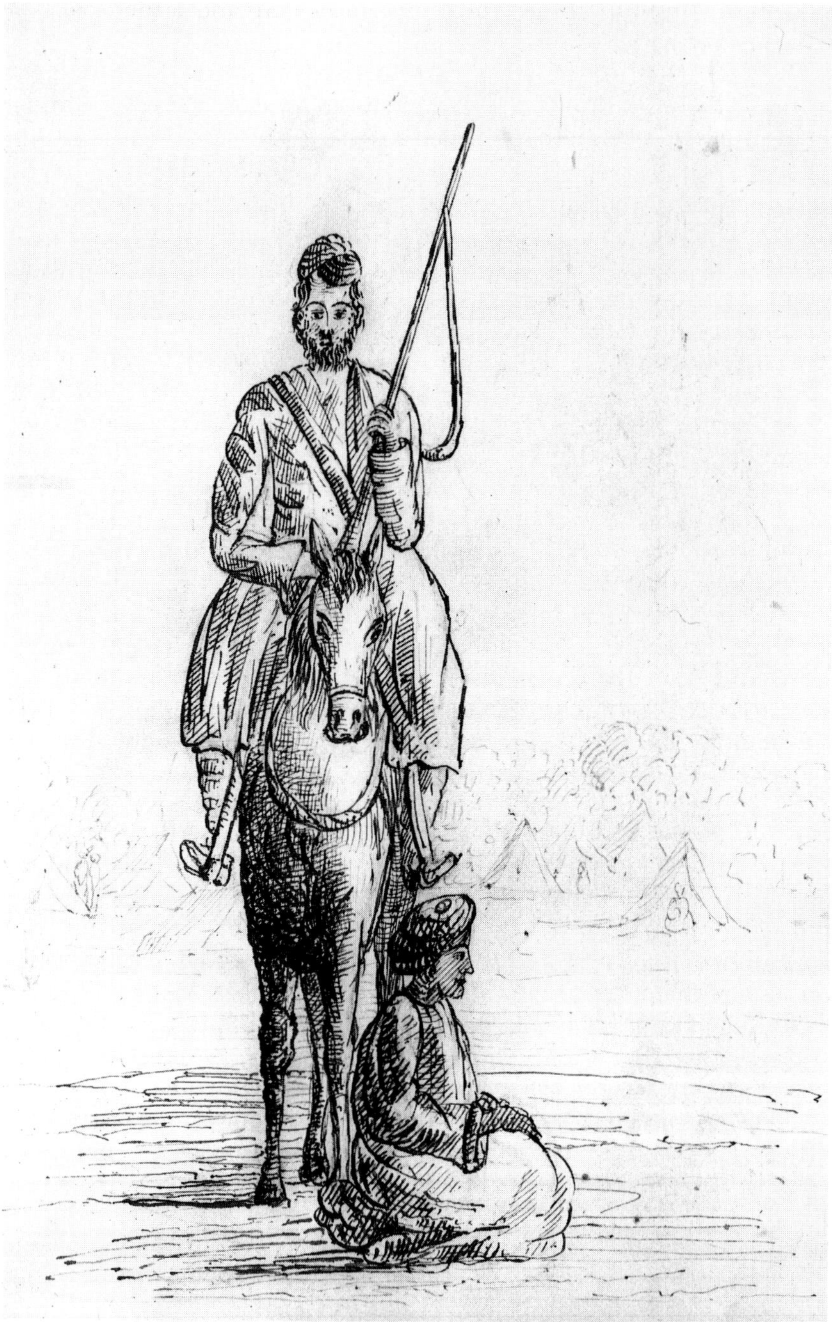

made him go about all the time in his lancer's cap and scarlet coat – he actually yawned with boredom.

Mr Macnaghten and Mr Torrens went today to see Shah Soojah's brother, the old blind king whose eyes were put out. How one would dislike one's fellow creatures in such a case.

November 19th

I believe till we reach Ferozepore a week hence we shall see nothing but a great sandy plain. However, the roads are improved. That man and that horse are part of William's standing army, which is composed of five such. In this country it is not safe to go out of the camp without attendants, but William's shooting and coursing propensities will not allow him to remain within it, so he has raised this force. But there is a combined movement this morning, three being sent to watch a sitting hare and a fourth to lead the greyhounds towards it. So this is the only standing army left. When on duty riding behind William they wear brown cowls like monks. He has made them all Field Marshals – Major Generals are so common here.

November 20th

We are encamped near the banks of the Sutlege today but we see nothing but sand. We should die of shock if we were to see anything else. I am low about sketching this year – this paper will not bear the coloured chalks – it grows rough if I rub them in. There are no buildings worth sketching and you know it is entirely the generosity of your nature which makes you guess that my figures are meant for figures, and my animals for animals. Not but what those bad dogs' heads are finished portraits of two of William's which ought to catch hares only they never find them, and those horses are very grand fragments – still I think I do buildings better. No wonder that I make grand fragments of horses' heads today, when for an afternoon's stroll we have been through I do not know how many lines of them, and as you know in this country they are nothing better or so good as regular wild beasts. But there are the artillery horses and the bodyguard horses and the escorts' horses and the muzzur horses (muzzur being the word we prefer here to presents and the horses, which have been given to us and which we are to give to Runjeet, being classically called muzzur horses) and some were muzzled and some were blinded and all were chained. I pottered by George's side in fear and trembling, feeling all the way as if they were biting each shoulder, and telling the fat officer who went with us how nice and pretty they looked.

November 21st. Ishara.
We came over dreadful roads again this morning. I hope Runjeet's roads will be better. He told Major Wade that he had made two new roads, not knowing which way George would come, but he thought road making was a foolish English custom – roads only served to shew your enemies the best way into your country. He sends here now every evening a hundred pots of sweetmeats which make the servants exceedingly happy.

I am rather unhappy about the state of our society just now. In this strange country we have three regiments with us instead of one, and though there is a certain degree of safety in not having the large durbar tent pitched every day, the tent that is pitched has the want of tact to hold twenty at dinner. And so besides all our own belongings, which are large, it is our bounden duty to have four or five officers every day. It must be an obliquity on my part but it strikes me that all those we have yet had are positive idiots – of course I only mean as far as conversation goes. I dare say they fight with the greatest genius. None of them can be made to speak at all. I know one reason is, they have been so long in the country and so used to smoke their hookahs, they are miserable without them, and it is not etiquette to smoke where George is. I am thinking of giving them a very large dinner in my own tent and letting them bring their own hookahs and then I shall see what they can say. There are our hackeries waiting to be loaded.

November 22nd. Dunhamkoteghoonie.

There is something attractive in the sweet simplicity of that name. Rolla and I have been passing a sad morning. A large black monkey of Captain Macintosh's got loose. I found my ayah in utter confusion, then discovered the monkey had been sitting on my dressing table looking at himself in the glass. He had made off with my pincushion and bit a man in the leg who tried to take it from him, jumping from one tent to another and pelting everybody with lumps of dust who tried to catch him. And Rolla moans and will not be comforted because he (Rolla) is shut up.

There are an unhappy band mounted on four elephants, great drum and all – four men on each elephant sitting back-to-back like people on a jaunting car, playing on their instruments with all their might and with great success, considering every step of every elephant shakes a note out of them. They are practising for the meeting with Runjeet! Chance's little elephant, being affected by the music, ran just now with pleasing playfulness at the four elephants and made them start back as they always do at a little animal, which produced a complete cessation of harmony . . .

I wonder what I would give to hear you talk to me for two hours! It is a thought which has just come over me. I should not amuse you, I fear. I am bored with being such a bore.

November 23rd. Tulwandee.

That on the other side is William showing Chance how to ride the little elephant [see p. 168]. He has got on one of those hats they make in the hills for shooting, covered with chicken's feathers – very light and they keep off the sun. I shall make a point of landing in one at Portsmouth.

Chance is grown a leetle fat since you last saw him. To be sure this Indian climate does strange things to people. When I went out to luncheon just now I found what I took to be a nice little child in a red coat playing about before the tent. However, he was introduced in form, and George and William began asking questions about Shah Soojah and Dost Mohamed's strength and victualling the army – as if he were a real man. It turns out that he is a most efficient officer. He said he

was suffering from the effects of the climate of Bengal. If it takes the dwindling line with us I shall insist on George's going home immediately. I never saw such a shocking little sight, and he is to help provide the victuals for 60,000 men – they will all be starved.

The mornings are bitterly cold now and we have the stoves lighted; and the afternoons are very hot and we have punkahs pulled. The thermometer varies forty degrees in six hours. That never happens in the hills.

November 24th

We do very short marches now, because we are not to get to Ferozepore before Runjeet does. My ayah, whose conversation is composed of a mixture of Irish brogue which she learnt from her husband and Hindustani idioms, says in her languid voice that makes me die of laughing: 'That black Rajah is a terrible fellow. He says that if any people sell us Europeans trinkets from his bazaar he will cut off their ears, and he keeps his mind so to himself that if his very best wife asks him a question he thinks impertinent he makes her pay him a lac of rupees. They tell me he is sick, really sick, if the grandson comes in his sight who is to have his throne when he dies. If you please I shall be glad to get out of this black Rajah fellow's kingdom.' In Bengal people are all 'wallahs', which means 'fellow', and it is not at all meant in a tone of reproach.

There has been a very pretty durbar today, one of Runjeet's chiefs with his followers. Their dresses are perfectly beautiful, though too much like people at Astley's.* The hangings of one of the elephants today looked as if they were made of solid gold. Loma Singh, the chief who came, is a great astronomer, and really very clever. George was very much struck by his manner and conversation, and he condescendingly observed when he came away that he had never met with a better mannered man than the Governor-General.

There are plenty of quails and black partridge to be shot today, and antelopes and hares for the greyhounds to course, so the camp may be pronounced in spirits. There were no pears for Rolla today. I knew there would be a catastrophe if they trusted that little man to victual the army.

November 25th, Sunday

We are at the same place we were yesterday, which makes it the more unlucky that I have never been able to catch what the name of it is. I have got a feeling upon me today that we have got into such completely different worlds it is utterly impossible we should ever meet again. On Sunday that feeling is always stronger upon me than on any other day. Mr Wimberley reads and preaches beautifully, but it never seems natural to go to church in a tent with all that sound of camels and elephants and heathen voices round – and the total absence of all women in the camp makes it look less natural still. I believe that at Ferozepore among 100,000 people we shall meet eight women, which we look upon as an extraordinary quantity.

Runjeet has sent forward 600 gardeners to make a garden round his

* Famous London circus

169

tent, as it is likely he will be kept there for ten days. I do not know how we shall keep up with that. I think we must say we hate the smell of flowers.

November 26th
We are only six miles from the town of Ferozepore. Where our camp is nobody seems exactly to know. I hope that we shall not go to Runjeet by mistake – it would put him out so and we might trample on his flower border . . . My dear, the Commander-in-Chief and all his staff are coming out to meet us tomorrow. I shall put on my cocked hat and feathers.

November 27th. Ferozepore.
We rode in yesterday without any of us being kicked off our horses, which I look upon as a blessing of a very peculiar kind. When one of the troopers' loose horses ran at Selim and me, he shewed a degree of self possession for which I can never sufficiently respect him.

You see we are again on an enormous plain – that is, we are let loose in India – three miles from the Sutlege, Runjeet encamped on the opposite bank, Sir Henry Fane encamped two miles nearer Ferozepore, and 'the army of the Indus' as we familiarly call the army which is to carry terror to the soul of Dost Mohamed, splashed generally about the plain. Kurruck Singh, Runjeet's heir, had been to a durbar this afternoon. Runjeet does not like him, which shows his usual discernment for by all accounts he is little better than an idiot in manner. Sir Willoughby Cotton (who will take the command when Sir Henry goes home until a successor comes), Macnaghten and William went on a visit of ceremony to Runjeet while Kurruck Singh came here. He kept them there drinking his strong wine and sent them back in a remarkable flow of spirits. The 600 gardeners had done their duty; there was a beautiful garden round his tent.

November 28th. Ferozepore.
I am reduced entirely to home sketching here. A sheet of sandpaper would beat any sketch I could make of the country round – it is just that – no trees, no hills, no nothing. The Sikhs are all picturesque and are willing enough to stand and be sketched, but I have not courage to do it for they laugh and observe to each other all the time and are very unlike the servile Bengalee race we live amongst. From so seldom seeing English people, our customs strike them as anything but sensible.

170

That bearer was standing between me and the sun when we were sitting before our tents and I have rather diminished the size of his umbrella. We think it very dignified to have large umbrellas and this one was made in the Pahalal Rajah's territories. It is painted all over flowers. If you want one, I'll speak to . . . about it [see p. 172].

George is making an immense piece of work in the street (we always talk of 'street of tents') with his levee, and we are going to have forty-five people at dinner today – the élite of the camp, chiefly composed of Major-Generals KCBs. We feel elated at this . . . prospect.

If you could only just see the shawls and gowns which came to us today strait from Cashmere! When General Allard was in Calcutta we commissioned him to order some. They are only just finished and now we must wear them and George must pay for them.

November 29th. Ferozepore.
We have had a very busy morning. The great durbar for the reception of Runjeet was at eight o'clock, that the troops might not be kept out in the sun. There was an immense shew of troops got up for him. George had to go to meet him on his elephant a little way from the camp. As usual the crush of elephants at the moment of meeting was awful. Nothing can prevent the mahouts on both sides from pressing their elephants to the last moment. However, George succeeded in transferring Runjeet from his howdah to his own without dropping him. He is so very little there might have been some danger of such a catastrophe.

We received him in the outer tent, and he sate down on the sofa between us with his legs tucked up. There was an immense rush of followers after him and it was some time before they would go out and get into order. Almost all his immediate courtiers have excellent manners, thoroughly gentlemanlike, making their topics through an interpreter. He himself does not wear a single jewel, but some of his favourites are covered with them and all their dresses are perfectly magnificent. He examines everything quite closely with his one eye and asks an infinity of questions. The long beard is as white as this paper. Emily, from the various prints of her, had painted a picture of the Queen in her coronation robes, which turned out successfully, and this was set in a large gold frame very much emeralded and diamonded and given to him. And it answered thoroughly. Sir W. Cotton brought it in and they all stood up and saluted . . . Runjeet said that when he got to his own camp and hung it up a salute of a hundred guns would be fired. Our presents to him have been very magnificent in the line of jewels, shawls, horses and cannon. There was one horse took him so much he

171

ran out into the sun to examine him, and a European man who took them to him had to ride them all before him for an hour and a half. He brought two little children with him, about five years old, a little boy and a girl, affianced to each other. They were orphans of his chiefs who had been killed in battle and he carries them about with him everywhere. They were tumbling about on the floor of the tent. George has to return his visit tomorrow.

November 30th. Ferozepore.
There is the very compendious method of watering the roads here. A bullock brings water in large skins and you go and fill small skins and squirt it out a few drops at a time. I see Miss Martineau* heading a chapter about it, 'Labour cheaper than carts'. I have been resting on my own today and have not much to say. Dr Drummond insists upon Emily taking a complete rest while she is here from all but the native shows. When I read the dinner list today, it made me very ill too – forty-five excellent officers whose names I have never heard before, except that dead-black Colonel Skinner, and he would not have sate next to me – not a single woman. So I went to George and showed him how much better they would all eat and drink in my absence, a fact which he is always slow about taking in. He has been returning Runjeet's visit this morning. Among the presents Runjeet gave are a large shawl tent and a silver bed, very much sprinkled with rubies and emeralds. I will tell you more about his tents tomorrow when he gives us an evening party.

December 2nd. Ferozepore.
I did not write yesterday, dear, because I had a deal to do. Runjeet was to give us a party at his tents. George, Macnaghten and William set off for a private conference at three, I followed them at five, Emily meaning to keep her strength for the great review tomorrow. Sir W. Cotton was to go with me and I set off with him and his aide-de-camps in the carriage and a squadron of lancers to guard us – very grand and dusty. We had to cross the Sutlege into Runjeet's territories and had to get upon elephants to go over the bridges of boats. The approach to the tents was beautiful. They were surrounded by a large enclosure of scarlet and embroidered cloth, the tents themselves made of shawls and embroidered cashmere and all his chiefs covered in jewels and armour, and shawl drapery. I was a little shy on my first arrival among the Singh family. However, Heera Singh, a boy who has great power over Runjeet, and

* (1802–76). Utilitarian social reformer

173

Sher Singh who is a great soldier and supposed to have an eye to the throne when Runjeet dies, talked very well through an interpreter. I was taken to a silver chair at the entrance of the tent where George and Runjeet and William were sitting, and in a few minutes they joined me. We were in a kind of open tent with silver pillars. It was soon filled with chiefs and nautch girls – in his troop of amazons as he calls them. I was disappointed in their beauty.

Runjeet's next step was to have a low solid gold table placed before him and two large gold branch candlesticks on the floor by it. The table was covered with gold bottles and cups and some specimens of Sikh cookery – spiced balls of meat, or rather essence of meat, of very strong composition, pomegranate seeds etc. There were two little ugly children as usual who serve Runjeet and me for our standing jokes. The composition he calls wine is like burning fire, much stronger than brandy, and his great delight when he sets in to be gay is to make people drink it. At first he was content with making George and Sir W. Cotton swallow it – or rather pretend to swallow it. Then he began plying me with gold cupfuls. I got on very well for some time, pretending to drink it and passing it to his cup-bearer. But he grew suspicious, put it up to his one eye, looked well into the cup, shook his head and gave it me back again. The next time he put his finger into the cup to see how much was gone. I made Major Wade explain to him that ladies did not drink so much in England, upon which he watched till George's head was turned away and passed a cup to me under his arm, thinking George was the horrid tyrant who prevented me. Fireworks were going all round us and nautch girls dancing before us all the time we were there. I got him to show us his 'Sea of Light',* a diamond out of which he starved Shah Soojah. It is as large as a small egg. Some of the emeralds he showed us at the same time are quite wonderful and I hope he came by them honestly.

In the course of the evening they brought the king a neat little tray and he took diamond bracelets from it and put them on my arms, and a large diamond ring which he put on my finger, and a large string of pearls which puzzled us both dreadfully to get over my bonnet. I went in a bonnet because though the Sikhs think very ill of us for appearing at all, they would think still worse of us if we were to appear with our heads uncovered. When Runjeet's countenance lights up he is very clever. Otherwise he sits like a little old grey statue. We left him still drinking when we came away and we were not left with the impression that the Sikhs lead strictly moral lives.

* The Koh-i-nor, now part of the British Crown Jewels

December 4th. Ferozepore.

We have been this morning to see a review of the ten thousand troops which are going to Cabul, just the sort of sight that interests Runjeet Singh. We went to it on our elephants. I hung back while he and George met, for the crush is sometimes awful. Captain Cunningham's elephant died after the last meeting – did not live an hour. This was just the sort of sight to interest Runjeet and listening to the questions he had interpreted, I was more struck by his cleverness than I had been before. The instant we got near the troops he was like a child within sight of a new plaything. He rode up the whole line, near three miles, examining them all. I made that sketch of him from my elephant as he sate on his horse seeing the troops pass, and it is supposed to be very like him [see p. 176]. He stoops quite as much. He would not let Dhian Singh or Sher Singh, who are supposed to have a hope of the throne when he dies, have a near view of the troops and ordered them away from them. The ground was a beautiful sight, all his wild looking Sikhs about, Skinner's Horse making a charge with their war cry, and such a mass of elephants with those chiefs covered with jewels seated on them. We gave our European brethren a breakfast in a tent pitched on the ground, and I am rather tired at this present writing. I did not tell you yesterday that the man was killed who was taking the letters of the camp – 'the post', in short. The letters have been found today at some distance from him. Now and then jewels are sent by post and I wonder such a catastrophe has not happened oftener.

December 5th. Ferozepore.

We have been giving a return nautch party to Runjeet, and it is all over by eight, so I will write this before I go to bed. But it was so like the one he gave us, I need not say much about it. We had one of the 'gardens of light' made before the tent where he was to sit. Captain Cunningham who was laying it on, said in a melancholy tone, 'I doubt having enough lamps for my garden.' I asked him how many he had put down – 51,000. As there were besides a mass of carts full of fireworks I ventured to suggest that might do. It was a trying moment when I had to give Runjeet an emerald ring – a single emerald so large it reached to the first joint of my finger, and I could not get a glove over it. If it had had any tact it would have refused to come off at all. The nautch girls' singing generally runs to screaming, and I do not think I ever heard anything like it last night. We stopped there for a time and let our own band play but he begged to have the singing again. There was rather a longer pause than usual and I heard Macnaghten translating for George's

pleasure, 'My Lord the Maharajah says he wishes your lordship would give him a little more friendly conversation.' So pleasant when he had actually exhausted himself.

December 6th

I was beat about sketching yesterday. I could not find a single tempting article and today does not look promising. We have crossed the river today and are in the Punjaub, Runjeet and his camp three miles from us. George does not come until the afternoon. He stays on pretence of business with the other camp, but I have an idea that he has sold Emily, William and me for slaves, that his companions are now breaking up the bridge of boats and he himself is on his way to Calcutta. I don't envy him his feeling when he saw us set off. I went to his tent at seven o'clock, and he pretended not to be dressed. No wonder he could not bear the sight of us.

Runjeet had a review of his troops yesterday and all our people are in astonishment at his state of discipline, and the very superior way in which they performed their manoeuvres. I did not go myself because without a day's rest I had not strength of mind or body to swallow another bit of elephant or Sikh, but I have a notion from what I can gather that our review was a remarkably poor piece of business, compared to theirs. William and I rode through a bit of their camp this morning and they were very quiet but I am rather afraid of them.

December 7th

There are no roads for a carriage here so Emily took to her palanquin this morning – and I went with George and William on elephants half-way, and rode the rest. Runjeet has sent his son, Sher Singh, to go with the camp, which is an odd measure, for he [Runjeet] is generally very jealous of his [Sher Singh's] avowed taste for the English. He copies our customs as far as he knows them – dines off English plate and uses knives and forks. Sher Singh came with us this morning and is a most theatrical looking personage, with excellent manners. At that early hour, his turban was covered with emeralds and pearls, he was in a scarlet pellisse embroidered with gold, and the trappings of his horse and his elephant were magnificent. His followers are fine wild looking people. He is a great sportsman and his hawkers follow him, and he carries an English double-barrelled gun. He bore with great philosophy seeing me ride, and would only note the difference of habits. It is rather a blow to me that he has invited himself to dinner. He has evidently an idea that the Singhs and the Edens should live together as one family. Though he is very intelligent and laughs heartily at any joke, it is always a *gêne* talking through an interpreter. He has picked out one of the aide-de-camps who is an artillery officer, and another belonging to the engineers, to talk over military matters with him.

December 8th

We have had a very long march this morning; they say nearly twenty miles, but then the distances cannot be measured. They would be jealous of a perambulator going over their country. I came all the way riding either a horse or an elephant, before breakfast, and am pretty tired at this present writing. Sher Singh – or as we call him in company, 'The King's prince' – came with us. We had a great deal of hawking on the road and every now and then he and his spearmen and followers set off at full gallop after some shot; he is a wonderful shot himself. He led William such a life because he had not brought his gun after he had challenged him the evening before, and declares the forfeit was a dozen of wine and insists upon having it. He and two followers sate through our dinner yesterday. He only drank and would not hear of eating. He talked really very cleverly, and is fond of drawing. We have been obliged to insinuate through Major Wade that we do not wish him to break through his customs every evening in our favour, though we hope he will come to us sometimes.

Runjeet only left this ground just before we came up to it. He feeds us all, to the lowest camp followers. Nothing is allowed to be bought in the bazaar, and with three regiments you may conceive the expense. There is a hookabadar by his fire this evening [see p. 155].

December 9th, Sunday

We have not moved today. The Maharajah sent word, he knew it was not our custom to travel on Sundays so he had provided two days' provisions. The united sense of all the political agents has been put together to stop this provisioning system. With three regiments in addition to the usual number of camp followers, I am afraid to say how many thousand people are to be fed, and it must be a heavy burden on Runjeet's chiefs and people, though he does not care himself. Moreover it is a point of conscience to make the soldiers and servants indent for only strict necessities, and as they are all well paid they would rather be allowed to have what they like and pay for it. However, it turns out to be the custom to feed allies who march through the kingdom, and it would be considered a national disgrace to do otherwise. The very fire wood we burn is sent to us, and as I never see a tree I want to ask Runjeet confidentially where it comes from.

Sher Singh invited himself again to dinner yesterday. George will not see the proceeding in the heinous light I do. You understand it is impossible to eat and talk through an interpreter. He brought his son, Pertaub Singh, a little boy only seven years old, very slender and graceful, in a gold cloth dress and all his father's jewels upon him as well as his own. I never saw anything so splendid. He had a little sword, and matchlock too, and shoots as well as any of them. His Sikh tutor stood behind him. The boy has a teacher to learn English and asked two or three times for the Padre Sahib – Mr Wimberley. I shewed him that sketch of Runjeet and he clapped his hands and said 'My grandfather'. He seems to have some notion of drawing himself. This afternoon Sher Singh brought his little dog – you never saw such a little fat thing – naturally white but painted scarlet, two or three rows of pearls round its neck and a large emerald bandeau round its head. Chance felt hurt that he had none. Nothing could be more polished than Rolla's manner was, considering the visit was partly to him, though he was bored to death and longing to run up the tent ropes. He sate in Sher Singh's arms with his two arms on his shoulders, with the most exemplary patience, without making war between the natives by giving him a bite, which I fully expected. I think in this strange country he must be allowed an escort to follow his palanquin.

December 10th
These are two of Runjeet's irregular horsemen – they were standing before our door just now. There was nothing very striking about them but I am obliged to take what comes in the way [picture not included]. As to doing horses, I can't – and the horses in this country are either the gigantic Persian horses which look unnatural or those long-backed creatures which might be called mules, only they are horses. So if I were to do them ever so well, you might be misled into thinking them failures and that would be a pity.

George and William have been out shooting with Sher Singh – just as you would naturally stroll out for an afternoon's shooting in England – on elephants with horsemen riding about and peeping into every bush till they catch the eye of a sitting animal, and then they point it out and then everybody shoots at once, and then they bring it to the Lord Sahib and say it is his. Before they set off, a squadron of horse had been sent out to look for the hares.

Now there is Captain MacGregor come to say that another Sikh chief – a great astronomer – wants Rolla sent to his camp. He shan't go. They will say he is a comet and try experiments with his long tail.

December 11th
We are within five miles of Amritsar today and they have made us encamp here that George and Runjeet may do something royal and grand about entering tomorrow. In the meantime, neighbour Singh has been dining with us again. We are getting to look upon him quite in that light, though I still take pains to impress upon George a fact about which he is totally unpersuadable, that he would be less trouble to us at any other time than at dinner. He was in a high state of exultation about his own shooting today. When he asked William to drink some wine with him he added 'For though God has not given Captain Osborne the gift of shooting, perhaps he has of drinking wine'. He brought poor little Pertaub's intended father-in-law with him: I do not think that

little Mrs Pertaub will be allowed much of her own way. I never saw such a little sharp creature as he is, though kept in great awe by his father. I do not know how many hundred baskets of fruit and vegetables Runjeet sent into camp today.

December 12th. Amritsar.

My dearest, if you could but have seen the splendour of the sight we saw this morning, you would simply have died of it. As it is, you will only turn sleepy over the description. But I think that the entrance to the camp this morning was the finest thing I ever saw anywhere. There were altogether four miles of Runjeet's soldiers drawn up in lines. We passed through a mile-and-a-half of them – his bodyguard. A great number of these are uniformly dressed in bright orange turbans, tunics and trousers, the others provide their own dresses for which they have an enormous allowance. They are all of the same form, made of 'kincob' – gold and silver . . . cloth of every possible shade of colour. They have long black or white beards half down to their waists and a large expenditure of shawls and scarves disposed in drapery about them. Their matchlocks are inlaid with gold or steel or silver, and some of them with bows and arrows, some with long spears, and all the chief ones with . . . black heron's plumes. Everything about them is showy and glittering – their horses with their gold or silver hangings, their powder flasks embroidered with gold.

They are a fine looking people by nature but keep every member of the camp in a constant state of pique with their conceit. The aide-de-camps are in a state of fret about it. The Sikhs laugh at their tailless horses, ask them what they receive as their pay, shrug up their shoulders and say 'What a paltry sum', and name six times as much for their own receipts – not the least true generally these, the servants say. They are so tiresome talking of their cities and their Maharajah. 'We tell them, come to our Calcutta and we shew you plenty of fine things there you never saw.' In the meantime, they are all remarkably civil. Although nobody stirs from the camp without guards of some kind, they hardly seem to be necessary.

There are some excellent shawls to be bought here. If I had not spent so much of your money lately, I should have been much tempted to make you buy a real good shawl. I am sure that for £30 here I could get you as good a one as you pay £80 for in England. But Runjeet puts an enormous duty upon any article brought from the city and it is very difficult to find any merchant who will come to the camp.

180

December 13th. Amritsar.

We are to stay here for a few days. This morning I got your letter number 33 – born in Scotland, carried on in London, finished at Motcombe and then quite naturally fulfulling its vocation in Amritsar. It's odd, but a halo of mystery still hangs over the fate of your bracelet. I shall not give either you or myself a moment's peace till I hear the truth of that. We are going into the city this afternoon and I am cut short, so I shall say more about number 33 tomorrow.

December 14th. Amritsar

We did a great deal yesterday afternoon. Runjeet came at 3 o'clock to fetch George, and as usual they got into one howdah, a solid gold one, Macnaghten as interpreter running his elephant on one side and Emily and I as his appendages running ours on the other, and a great crush of elephants behind, and an awful crush it is sometimes. I did not hear of it at the time but William saw yesterday one elephant driver completely flattened between two elephants. He seems to have died instantaneously but it is a frightful kind of death.

There is a fort where all Runjeet's treasures are kept in subterranean places, but he will not let any of us go into that. I own that I should like to take a hand candlestick and have a good look after what he has got. Half his tributes are paid in jewels. The city is a poor looking city, but it was a curious sight to pass through, from the immense throng of people from the ground to the top of the houses – a great number of nautch girls weighed down with the trinkets they are loaded with.

Our object was the great Sikh temple, where the book he consults as an oracle is kept. We had all to take off our shoes before we entered even the outer court. Emily and I astutely had our slippers over white satin shoes, and they were quite satisfied when our slippers were taken off. It was getting dusk and the whole city was illuminated. The temple itself was sheeted with gold, the whole outside of it, good solid gold, and a very large building. Runjeet was afraid I should not make that out as I was standing near the door, and took hold of my hand and made me feel it. The inside of the temple is more splendid still – a large gold canopy stiff with embroidery in pearls.

There is the oracle with about twenty covers over it, and priests with long white beards sitting behind a little low altar on which it is kept. Chouries are wound over it. A very small round cushion was put on the ground, upon the edge of which Runjeet instantly squatted. He pulled down George by him, also Emily and me. It was very close sitting and rather crampy. He evidently thought that women wanted something to

181

amuse their little trivial minds, and made signs for us to go up to the altar and look at the book. A fringe of very long pearls and emeralds about half a yard deep and a yard long is the first covering. Then the priests take off many more and there was the book open and they all bowed to it. I rather felt as if I was in the temple of Baal. I hear Runjeet told George that in consequence of coming to see that sacred place he should consider their friendship more firmly cemented, and George made a most splashy answer, about their united armies conquering the world. You will be much taken aback, I guess, when they march hand in hand and take Motcombe. Then Runjeet told us a long story how his oracle first told him to make friends with the English. I wish somebody could have sketched us all three, with the mixture of natives and English officers round us, half kneeling, half squatting.

Afterwards we went to the top of a building near, to see the illumin-ations, and the gold temples looked splendid with the reflection of the fire.

These are two Akalis. Major Wade just brought two of them to be sketched. They are the most lawless people here. There was a time when they used to insult Runjeet in every possible manner and he bore it, for they are kinds of priests as well as soldiers and ruffians. Now he has tamed many of them and these belong to his regular army, but still wear their odd coarse blue dresses and carry their own arms – sharpened quoits, swords, and pistols in profusion. Very wild-looking creatures they are, and insult almost everybody that passes them . . .

December 15th. Amritsar.
I was idle this morning and did not get up to go to a review of Runjeet's troops when George set off at sunrise. But after breakfast I set off in the carriage after them, meaning to drive near and see the end of it; a large number of wild looking Sikhs galloping round the carriage by way of protection and 'Sergeant' . . . , as our stable man is called, riding by the side by way of interpreter. After going for four or five miles promis-cuously over the country and seeing nothing, I ventured to ask where the review was. The Sikhs answered innocently that they did not know. I asked where they were taking me. They said to Runjeet's camp. It struck me as a bold measure. However it was too late for the review, and I let them take their own way, and we drove strait through it. He had 30,000 troops out that day, and their tents of all sorts of colours covered an immense space of ground. Nothing could be quieter or civiller than the people about the camp, the sentinels all presenting arms as the carriage passed . . .

December 16th, Sunday. Amritsar.
Little Pertaub came to have his picture drawn. Nothing could be prettier
than his dress: his turban bright green gauze cashmere, his trousers and
tunic a kind of very thick bright green satin, a loose yellow satin pelisse
stiffly embroidered with silver, and the usual quantity of pearls and
large emeralds. His sword, shield, and matchlock he insisted on having
put in. He is really a wonderfully clever child, with excellent manners.
He orders his servants about with much majesty, but was very respectful
to his old Sikh teacher who came with him today. Emily made a very

good picture of him. That sketch is like him. He has such enormous black eyes, they are almost unnatural. Runjeet gave us another of his nautches last night, exactly on the pattern of the one I described before, except that he drank harder himself and got very drunk, and tried hard to make George drink. 'When a man drinks hard enough,' he said, 'he opens his heart and talks all kind of nonsense, and that is right among friends.' He asked if it was true that books are written against drinking, shook his head and said what foolish books they must be.

December 17th

We have moved ten miles today – four marches will take us to Lahore. Sher Singh is turning into a great . . . When the Maharajah is present he never dares open his lips. Our servants grow more unhappy every day at the way the Sikhs laugh at their ways and our ways. Ariffe nearly cried because they offered him water to drink out of his turban, saying that stiff thing could be meant for nothing else. The plot against Rolla's liberty is thickening, and more messages had been sent for him, to which he sent dignified refusals. Today a large circle of Sikhs are sitting outside my tent. Asked what they wanted, they said to make their salaams to the Hounymann, which means a sacred monkey. Major Wade says he is in grave danger of being stolen. Of course we shall waive all personal considerations and declare war against Runjeet at once if that were the case.

It has suddenly struck me that if Runjeet were to die we should all be in a great scrape. Each Sikh who wanted a bit of the kingdom would seize one of us as a hostage. Mind, if they do, that you do nothing foolish in England likely to affect the Sikhs.

December 18th

Ten miles we have come today and at breakfast all the people who rode on one side of the canal said what a beautiful state of cultivation the country was in, and all the people who rode on the other said what a pity to see so much waste-land. So now you know the state of things exactly . . .

Runjeet, in a transport of confidence and friendship, took George and all who chose to go into the fort of Govindghur which he had never before allowed a stranger to enter. The Sikh soldiers say that now there is no doubt that the Sikhs and English are one family or the Maharajah would never have done such a thing. It seems to be the sort of fort that you and I could take – weak but pretty to look at, and full of treasure and jewels. I am thinking of some strengthening messes that I could send the Maharajah – now I have got that hostage notion in my head, I am in such a fright he should die.

Another bad incident is that when Dr Drummond came to dinner last night he said a man had been bit by a mad dog . . . Two hours after, a servant of Mr Torrens was bit at the door of his tent, and an hour later another man in one of our servants' tents, and the dog is still about, and as hundreds of pariah dogs follow the camp half of them may be bit, and I expect we shall all be bit crossing from one tent to another. They are talking of having all the dogs killed, but that is a difficult operation, beside the horror of their dying howls. Each of the regiments have favourite pariah dogs attached to them, and it would not be a popular measure to kill them. George is making a close sort of reckoning that we shall recross the river in ten days and that no dog will go mad before that, and they will all be left on this side. I expect we shall all be in the last stages of hydrophobia by that time and refuse to cross the river.

December 19th. Shalimar.
I have found nothing to sketch for the last three days, but now we are encamped close by the Shalimar Gardens, and there are some promising-looking buildings in them. We are only four miles from Lahore.

My ayah has just told me with great triumph that being exceedingly provoked at the wonder the Sikhs express at the open manner in which we walk about the world, she told them yesterday that Emily and I are two very powerful Begums, who can give themselves permission to do anything. 'And that seemed to strike them dumb.'

The dogs all look particularly wild and eccentric today; they will be sure to bite us and all the camels before many days pass. I can imagine no more frightful thing than a mad Governor-General and his camp tearing wildly over the country. Emily is talking of returning to Simla three weeks hence, when George turns off for Agra; in which case we shall not get to Simla till after the hot winds set in in a month. A pleasant prospect.

December 20th. Shalimar.
We are halting because Runjeet is to give us a fête in the gardens tonight. I am shocked to say that I think George is getting rather fond of these drinking bouts. Runjeet gives him the example of talking a little nonsense sometimes at them, though they say much less than he used to do. The interpreters I imagine soften now and then questions that are

asked. He was telling George the other day it was very sad he had not one wife – the Sikhs had twenty-five. George said that in England they sometimes found one more than they could manage. At which Runjeet answered that if the women were troublesome, they beat them. I got Macnaghten to tell him that I wished he would not tell the Lord Sahib that which made him laugh violently – and he probably hopes that George is giving us a good beating today.

I went to the garden this morning and sketched that gateway. Nadir Shah* passed through it when he was going to conquer Delhi. There are great remains of magnificence but everything going to decay. The orange and lime trees are immense.

December 21st. Lahore.

Runjeet gave a very pretty fête in the gardens last night. I have sketched on the page beyond the building where we sate; shawl tents with gold and silver linings were pitched in it. From some mistake, there was not water enough for the fountains to play, and they had showers of fire from them, and all the gardens and buildings illuminated, and the reflexion in the water was beautiful. Some of Dost Mohamed's young brothers were there; they are at deadly feud with him and had fled to Runjeet. They put a tribute of money into his hand when they first came into the tent.

I never saw such a splendid mixture of dresses as were in that building last night. These Cabul princes in their loose dresses and turbans are quite unlike the Sikhs. There was a line of men in complete suits of armour guarding one of the doors. Some of the Sikh chieftains had natural flowers mixed with jewels in their turbans. The crowd of nautch girls came forward now and then, glittering with every kind of ornament.

This morning we came on elephants through the city. The few striking buildings that are left are beautiful from the remains of enamel upon them, the colour of the inlaid flowers quite as fresh as if it were just done. There is one mosque that is almost perfect still. Nothing can be more filthy than the city itself – narrow streets and certainly no scavengers. Before we entered it we went through a wilderness of ruined tombs, very picturesque. At one mosque we passed, a thousand Sikh priests are buried, martyrs to the Mahommedans who put them all to death because they would not change their religion. The principal priest was flayed alive. Runjeet went with us all the way. The people seem glad to see him, calling out 'Maharajah' and trying to catch his eye as he passes. We shall remain here for a week and then take leave of him.

* of Persia. Sacked Delhi in 1736.

December 22nd. Lahore.

Sher Singh came to be sketched today . . . but he would not sit still a minute. He had put on some beautiful jewels – a row across his shoulder of pear emeralds. We had him in Emily's tent. Five minutes after I thought he was gone, and had sent this book back to my tent, I got a message from William begging I would come directly. In my tent I found Sher Singh and all his Sikhs examining everything on the tables, and he with this book carefully tucked under his arm that he might take it away.

William and Captain Shewen, finding they could not get it from him, had sent for me. I should never have seen it again, for with much amiable savage playfulness he has a turn for appropriating any article he fancies. He would have got all this writing translated, and our heads would have been off next day. It was very difficult to put myself into a Persian passion. However, I explained through an interpreter that this is a private letter to somebody in England, and that in England people would be very much astonished if anybody in the Punjaub were to read private letters; it was against our custom. After a long while I got it.

December 23rd, Sunday. Lahore.

We were yesterday by way of seeing a review of Runjeet's bodyguard. We did hear a considerable quantity of firing, and sate in a shawl tent while it went on. Then they all came and rode past, Runjeet's own horses being led first, his favourite among them – a living mass of emeralds. He puts his very finest jewels on his horses, and the splendour of their harness and housings surpasses anything you can imagine. The emerald one they estimate at 30 lacs of rupees – £300,000 – and he begged George if he fancied any horse to take it as he stood. But he didn't. There was one with turquoise trappings I could have fancied myself.

All the Guchenas, as his guards are called, rode by. They all made their horses rear and beat their feet against the ground, and they brandished their spears. Some of the archer people with their bows and arrows are the most picturesque. When those dreadful Akalis passed, all Runjeet's chiefs quietly closed round the entrance of the tent. They made an immense noise, brandishing their swords, making their horses

189

kick, laughing violently and using the most abusive language, which Runjeet laughs at. Every chief that passed threw his tribute of a rupee.

Those two little ugly children he makes pets of were tumbling about the tent all the time. I do not believe they have been washed or dressed since we came into the country. We gave them some rupees for playthings.

Heera Singh, his prime minister's son, whom he makes a favourite of, came to see us today with an enormous escort. His father came at the same time to see George with only four followers. He, Dhian Singh, is a very superior man, mild and clever. He has two thumbs, which disturbs me.

December 24th. Lahore.
Now there, I said how it would be. Runjeet was to have had a review today, and it is put off because he is not well. When that is the case he sends for every doctor that can be found, and Dr Drummond has just been to see him and found him with eyes closed lying on a little low bench without curtains, and decidedly very feverish. So there we are at this present writing, nothing better than hostages. Dhian Singh will seize George, Kurruck Singh will seize William, Sher Singh Emily and Golaub Singh me, and when they march to fight for this kingdom we shall be put in front of their respective armies, so very possible and unpleasant. At the best we shall have to make forced marches to the river, leaving all our baggage behind us – and I bought such a lovely agate cup just now. I shall never have strength of mind to do that.

Runjeet sent his old faquir to Mr Wimberley to ask for two services to be translated into Persian for his special use – he was so anxious to know what we all do on a Sunday. I heard some horrors about some of his chiefs today. He never interferes with their possessions, and some of them commit all sorts of cruelties. Golaub Singh is *the* tyrant among them and it is a fact he has his dependants flayed alive and commits all sorts of cruelty of that kind. Runjeet himself is reckoned a model and does seem to be a kind-hearted old man now, whatever he was formerly.

We are to pay the principal Mrs Runjeet a visit before we go. Little Pertaub comes almost every day to sit through dinner with us, and has every merit in the world himself except talking English. But he has two tiresome old tutors and an aide-de-camp who stand behind him and try to make him talk of the garden of friendship, and everlasting affection etc., but his natural spirits get the better of them all.

I have been sketching Lahore from the plain, as you will see from the other side. If you could only see me at it. A very large quantity of Sikhs

besides our own sepoys is quite nice company. And an aide-de-camp and the tonjaun I am carried in and my elephant following, in case I should want it, and servants with silver sticks running on before. And so having set off to sketch in this sweetly simple manner, an immense crowd of Sikhs gather in two minutes, upon which the Sikh guards ride about with their long spears and make them all sit down. They draw round in two half circles, and everything is quiet and comfortable, much quieter than a set of little children in a village – unless a faquir comes whose trade is to abuse us at the full extent of his voice, and his abuse is sacred so nobody interferes. Before I finished this sketch there were some hundred Sikhs assembled, but they said nothing and did not laugh much.

We went yesterday to Jehan Gher's* tomb – an alarming expedition as we had to cross the river on elephants, and there were quicksands to pass over. The first elephant that passed over, they seemed to move from under him, so they beat the others to make them run over faster. I began to think that we should all sink, and Sher Singh the only one who had a black feather to leave behind. Jehan Gher's tomb has four minarets and inside and outside is inlaid with coloured stones in small patterns. It covers an enormous space of ground, but like all fine buildings in this country is going fast to decay. Little Pertaub, as he stood by the actual tomb inside the building, took a fit of moralising which rather scandalised his old tutors – 'I never saw this before and it is very fine, but of what use is it to the man who is here – what does he know about it? – there he is lying dead.'

* Jahangir, Mughal Emperor, 1605–27

December 25th. Lahore.
And so we have got to another Christmas day without having met – and one nearer meeting and I take comfort in that, dear, but somehow it is not natural to be passing Christmas here, and a strong wish for home comes over me. We have just come back from church, which the large tent is regularly called on Sunday, and it was full as it could hold – officers who have never seen a church for some years were there. We are colder here in tents than you can be by your fires just now in England. The thermometer was below freezing point this morning.

Runjeet is still very unwell today. The old faquir comes here two or three times a day to report about him, and evidently makes an excellent old nurse. Major Wade went to see Runjeet today – he found him very low about himself as he always is when he is ill, sitting up in his little room, the faquir squatting at his feet, the Prime Minister, Dhian Singh, standing, and his son, Heera Singh, Runjeet's favourite, seated in a chair by him. Dhian Singh is never allowed a seat. Heera Singh lives in much more state than either of Runjeet's sons, and has a very large military command though he is not yet twenty. He talks a great deal of English, and is constantly writing notes to William, beginning 'My dear Osborne' and 'My dear Friend'. His dress is always splendid. When George and Runjeet are in one howdah he sits behind and acts as Runjeet's interpreter.

If that sketch puzzles you it *must* be your own fault. I did it from the elephant the other day when we were crossing the river, and the elephant was rolling about like a ship at sea. A great many Sikhs were paddling themselves on inflated skins of pigs or young buffaloes. They shock all our Musselman servants here, for they shoot and handle and

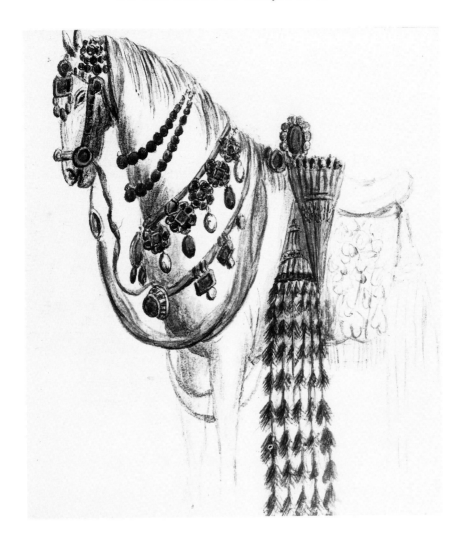

eat pigs . . . I am so cold. Be so good as to tell everybody that India is a very cold country.

December 26th. Lahore.
They brought five of Runjeet's horses here today for us to sketch, with all their jewels upon them. If ever we are allowed to plunder this kingdom, I shall go strait to their stables and the horses' trinket boxes. I sketched that one because he was the nearest to me, but all of them are

193

equally splendid. The emerald at his saddle is larger than the palm of my hand and those two rows round his neck are like overgrown grapes. The drop pearls and emeralds from the ruby necklace are magnificent, for all these are well cut fine coloured stones. Emily sketched another horse which had no other stones except emeralds on it, and there was one with a necklace made after the fashion of those bracelets (which I shall never know if you have got) which was nearly the death of us all with envy – each different stone so perfect and enormous. The holsters are of solid gold, and the saddle cloth is gold, and those tassel trappings are pretty. When you ride in the park I wish you would dress up your horse so. The sight of those jewels made me very ill. I coughed all night and could not sleep in consequence.

We none of us do anything but cough here, and no wonder, for we are encamped in the old bed of a river. Runjeet is still very unwell. He makes Dr Drummond send him medicines and takes a quarter of what he is meant to take.

December 27th. Lahore.

These are some people which come from Afghanistan and their camels are ornamented with bells and cowries sewn upon red belts. They have very odd matchlocks, as you see. We had rather an awkward scene with our friend Sher Singh last night. Having had our Xmas holiday, he was to come to dinner again. When I was going to the dinner tent I thought the aide-de-camp who came to meet me asked in a sinister tone whether Sher Singh had not come unexpectedly. However I answered a resigned No and went in. There I found him and Pertaub and the devoted tutors and two Cabul princes in their huge turbans – Dost Mohamed's brothers. My dearest, you must be an Indian cabinet minister to understand the full horror of such a proceeding: Dost Mohamed sitting upon the throne on which Shah Soojah is eventually to sit, and his two brothers brought in that neighbourly manner to see us eat our dinners. Sher Singh stepping forward quite delighted with his knowledge of English customs to wish me many happy Xmases.

I knew George had gone over but he had disappeared so I felt sure there was going to be a catastrophe. I had hardly intrenched myself on a sofa with little Pertaub when William came over to take me away. George had met Emily and stopped her, and then Mr Colvin had to explain to them that we could not receive uninvited guests in that way, and they all took to their elephants and went away, and India and dignity were vindicated and our soup was cold.

Sher Singh was not the least put out, for this morning when I rode with George to an inspection of the troops he came after us as usual, but he is not to be allowed to see us eat for the next three days at least.

December 28th. Lahore.

Now here's a blow to me. They are going to send off our letters for the next overland dispatch in four days, little more than a fortnight since they sent the last – such a want of consideration and this book not half done. But I will trick them and have it cut in two and send it all the same . . .

We have been today to the Palace to see a select number of Mrs Runjeets. The entrance to the Palace is very fine. George went over there before us, and in a small inner court in a small room we found him and Runjeet at a private durbar, Runjeet very feeble and looking very ill. There is a piece of water with fountains and a little palace in the middle of it for Runjeet's ducks, which now and then come at a waddle over the Cachemire carpets.

We went in there for five minutes. Then we were led off by Kurruck Singh, the eldest son, and Heera Singh, the favourite, to the ladies' apartment. They were in a wretched little room with a high wall before it. Two of the ayahs met us at the door and smeared us with attar, to the utter destruction of my bonnet and gown. They were all young, one of them really beautiful and very fair, the others very humdrum, the principal one a monster of fat. They had enormous nose-rings, their foreheads almost hid with jewels, silver gauze veils, tinselly tunics and very tight trousers.

Kurruck Singh informed us three times that *his* mother was dead, and Heera Singh said there were many more wives in the other rooms – these were all lawfully married. They asked a great many childish questions, and laughed violently when they took courage to look at us. We could not make out what their amusements are. I fancy they sleep away a great deal of their time. It does strike me, every time I see them, that their lives must be quite unbearable. The other day, General Ventura's little daughter came to see us. He has been in England lately, I think – one of Runjeet's French generals. When he got a chance to go home his child was kept here as a hostage. She is only eight years old and cannot speak a word of French but was dressed in a sort of European dress. The native mother has fattened her up to an enormous size. She is never allowed to take exercise and seems to live as one of themselves. All those French officers of Runjeet's have miserable lives of it, in fact. Those who first entered his service were enormously paid for a time. As he grows older he grows more avaricious every day, and now their pay is very low. They get a great many bad shawls to make up the right sum.

196

Sher Singh by Emily Eden

December 29th. Lahore.
It is raining hard which is very unpleasant. Rolla takes the best armchair and the best place by the fire and holds his hands out to the flame which would burn any Christian's. This is the day we ought all to take leave of Runjeet, but I cannot go out in the rain so Emily shall take leave for both. Tomorrow, you know, is Sunday. If you forget it and do not go to church, it is not my fault as I have told you. Next day we march, and so this journal will just finish off our Sikh bit of life.

197

December 30th, Sunday. Lahore.

After church today we went to pay a visit to Mrs Sher Singh, much the most interesting native visit we have paid in that line. She has come from some distance to meet us. She could not come to our tents, they are too open, but Sher Singh had one pitched near us. We were received with great state, a salute fired, all his household troops drawn up in their splendid dresses and Cachemire carpets covering the entire enclosure. The tent was very large, made of scarlet shawls. We left Major Wade and the aide-de-camps in the outer room. Sher Singh and little Pertaub took us into the inner one, which was very like an English drawing room – eight large glass windows, table covered with all kinds of bijouterie, for he gives large commissions to the French officers. The table covers of different coloured velvets embroidered with gold. Upon a large table an immense silver dinner service was put out, another was covered with perfumes and musical boxes of every size and shape.

His two ranees came in followed by Pertaub's old nurse. His mother is really beautiful; very little, very fair, with enormous black eyes and a pretty, clever expression. The other one's nose-ring was so enormous and had such large fringes of jewels hanging from it, it covered her mouth and half her face. They both talked merrily, and except that they stood up whenever Sher Singh moved, did not sound in awe of him; and both seemed equally fond of Pertaub, who shewed off all the English he had picked up. They made a very pretty picture of an eastern family. Sher Singh had made himself more magnificent even than usual, and his dress is always studied and graceful. He always wears what is called here the Choga – a shawl pelisse very loose and thick, embroidered with gold and silver.

The women were quite unlike any others we have seen, so coaxing in manner to us. I am always curious to know what they do to amuse themselves, but it is impossible to find out. They gave us I do not know how many trays of shawls and jewels, and we must borrow some of them to wear tonight when Sher Singh comes to dinner. He makes up violently always to English people since we have been here. Runjeet has brought Kurruck the eldest son much more forward than he ever did before, and of course he will naturally succeed to the throne. But Sher Singh, the second son, being cleverer and more popular, has always been suspected of wishing to supplant him. It is supposed that Runjeet has given him the office of marching with our camp in order to make him unpopular with the Sikhs, who do not all approve of his devotion to us.

In five days we shall recross the river and be in our own territories again. I think we are all left with a great respect for Runjeet's talents in the peculiar line of governing Sikhs.

December 31st

I must put this up today. The end of another year, and I ought to write that date only once more before we return to England. We have left Lahore and in five days shall take leave of all our Sikhs. Sher Singh goes with us till we recross the river. I wonder whether this will reach you in any shape at all, going by post; and if the Whigs should be out, Mr Smith* will have to pay a thousand guineas for it at least, which perhaps it is hardly worth. I think, though, that it will arrive too early in the year for a crisis. This is a very long letter, so goodbye and God bless you dearest.

Yours most affectionately
F. H. Eden

---

* Smith, Elder & Co, the London publishers, acted as agents for Waghorn's overland postal service to the East, via Suez. See footnote on p. 41.

Epilogue

By April 1839, the Governor-General's party was back in Simla once more, taking refuge from the hot weather. Ranjit Singh eventually succumbed to his outrageous lifestyle and died in June. His death, like that of Alexander the Great, was to reduce his kingdom to chaos. Kurruck Singh succeeded him, only to be deposed and (probably) poisoned in 1840 by his son, who was himself then killed by a falling archway. In 1843 Sher Singh was murdered by Ajit Singh who in turn was killed by Heera Singh. Dhian Singh had been killed on the same day as Sher Singh. Heera Singh was to perish in 1844. The Sikh Empire was finally absorbed into British India in 1849.

The expedition to Kabul continued in spite of Ranjit's death and by August Shah Shuja was installed in Dost Mohammed's place. The apparent success of the enterprise was marked by George being created an Earl. Life went on at Simla as in the previous year. Emily wrote: 'Everybody has been pleased and amused except two clergymen who are here, and who have begun a course of sermons against what they call a destructive torrent of worldly gaiety. They had much better preach against the destructive torrent of rain which has now set in for the next three months . . . Our parties begin at half-past eight, and at twelve o'clock we always get up and make our courtesies, and everybody goes at once. Instead of dancing very time, we have had alternations of tableaux and charades, and the result has been three aides-de-camp engaged to three very nice English girls, and the dismissal of various native Mrs Aides-de-camp . . .' Fanny took up carving dolls from wood for sale at the charity bazaar.

In November it was time to move down to Agra. George planned to spend some time there, supervising in particular the establishment of new schools. In the event their stay was cut short because of trouble over the opium trade in China. They were back in Calcutta by March 1840 so that George could superintend measures to see that this vital market for one of the mainstays of the Indian economy was kept open.

In 1841 Fanny suffered from weakness and continued exhaustion. To recruit her strength, she went on a trip by steamer for a few weeks. 'I think those great war tea-kettles, which go rolling on through storm and calm, wonderful inventions,' she wrote to Eleanor Grosvenor. 'The paddles are not irritating, and though the powder magazine was under my cabin, and cannon-balls would break loose and run about the deck, that was preferable to the noise of ropes and the creaking of bulkheads. A gale of wind to which, now it is over, I can never be sufficiently obliged, made us put in to the Prince of Wales Island – the most beautiful sample of an island you can fancy and with a hill where the climate is perfect. And there I remained instead of going on to Singapore. They gave up the Government House to us . . . We were chiefly waited upon by convicts, some branded on the forehead for murder. But it was the sin of their youth, and we were evidently expected to think it venial . . .'

The situation in Kabul was bad. In Christmas 1840 there had been an insurrection, and things got steadily worse through 1841. By the end of that year, Macnaghten and Burnes had been murdered and the remaining 4,500 British troops and sepoys started their retreat in January 1842. They and 12,000 camp followers were virtually all killed by the Afghans or the cold. George's misreading of the situation in 1838 finally had brought its reward.

At home, a Tory government had succeeded the Whigs and a Tory Governor-General had been appointed. The Edens left India in March, 1842, and reached England after a four months' voyage. Both sisters were very tired, and Fanny, in particular, had grown a good deal older than her years. Back in London, she and Emily settled in Eden Lodge, a charming house they had long since bought in Kensington (its site is now occupied by the Royal Geographical Society), but Fanny was not to enjoy it for long. She died in 1849, aged 48. George had died a few months before. Emily survived until 1869, publishing a novel, *The Semi-Detached House*, in 1859. Its success encouraged her to publish a second, *The Semi-Attached Couple*, written thirty years before. In 1866 her own account of the trip to Ranjit Singh, *Up The Country*, appeared. It is Emily, with her intellect and strong political sense, who compels respect. It is Fanny, who noticed everything and instinctively responded to human needs, who is best at sharing the pleasures of her travels.